Reminiscences of a Private

Reminiscences of a Private

William E. Bevens
of the First Arkansas Infantry,
C. S. A.

Edited with an Introduction by
Daniel E. Sutherland

The University of Arkansas Press • Fayetteville

1992

96   95   94   93   92   5   4   3   2

This book was designed by Chiquita Babb using the Bembo typeface.

The paper used in this publication meets the minimum requirements of the American National Standard for Permanence of Paper for Printed Library Materials z39.48-1984. ∞

Library of Congress Cataloging-in-Publication Data

Bevens, William E., 1841–1924.

    Reminiscences of a Private: William E. Bevens of the First Arkansas Infantry, C. S. A. / edited with an introduction by Daniel E. Sutherland.

        p.   cm.

    Rev. of: Reminiscences of a Private, 1914.

    Includes bibliographical references.

    ISBN 1–55728–223–4

    1. Bevens, William E., 1841–1924. 2. Confederate States of America. Army. Arkansas Infantry Regiment, 1st—Biography. 3. United States—History—Civil War, 1861–1865—Personal narratives, Confederate. 4. Arkansas—History—Civil War, 1861–1865—Personal narratives. 5. Soldiers—Arkansas—Biography. I. Sutherland, Daniel E. II. Title

E553.5.1stB48 1992

973.7′467′092—dc20

[B]   91-16519

                                              CIP

For Kim and Christopher

Contents

One of the last-known copies of these reminiscences, written by W. E. Bevens and originally published by him in book form, belongs to Edwin Chaney, great-grandson of Private John Cathey, Company G, First Arkansas. The pages are loose and yellowed with age. Years ago Chaney's grandmother (who was also Private Cathey's daughter) made a dust jacket from shelf paper to preserve the pages that contained her father's memories and part of a nation's history. The book has been made available now, by the Chaney family, in honor of the Confederate soldiers of Arkansas, in the conviction that the story it tells ought to be preserved for future generations.

John Griffin
Searcy, Arkansas
Robert C. Newton Camp 197
Sons of Confederate Veterans

Introduction

The Reminiscences

In 1927, Stephen Vincent Benét was hard at work on his epic narrative poem about the Civil War, *John Brown's Body*. In weaving his tale, Benét wanted to be as accurate as he could about the details of the war. He wanted to know what happened when, who said what to whom, what people felt and did in the great upheaval. The more he read about the war, however, the less certain he became of the facts. He had devoured scores of books on the subject; yet, as frustration mounted, he wished he had "a million more." He especially wanted firsthand accounts of the war: the words and the insights of the people who had been there and who had lived through the times. Then, having blurted out his wish, Benét became more circumspect. He considered the problems of interpretation that already bedeviled him, the trials he had already undergone in separating fact from fiction. No, on second thought, he did not want a million more books. "I am having trouble enough with the ones I can use," he confessed,"—people lie so, especially when they write their reminiscences."[1]

Every student of the war can sympathize with Benét, but it is evident that the poet had not read the reminiscences of William E. Bevens. Had he done so, he may have had a higher opinion of the genre. Considering the war as a whole—its width and breadth, the mighty resources devoted to it—Bevens witnessed only a tiny part of the bigger show. Yet, what he saw, what he experienced, and what he felt, he recorded faithfully. His errors are honest mistakes, and not very serious. One interesting, and clearly conscious, error concerns his military rank. Bevens served as a corporal for nearly a year after his enlistment in May 1861. Yet, in the years after the war, when so many Confederate veterans were elevating themselves to majors and colonels, Bevens preferred to be remembered as a lowly yet loyal private. Elsewhere in his narrative he misses a date from time to time. He sometimes confuses names, forgets details, or remembers an event differently from the way it occurred. But there are no wholesale lies, no dramatic fabrications. He tells the truth, mostly.

His is also a very personal account of the war. Bevens is not introspective or philosophical. He rarely dwells on the large issues of the war. He had wide experience in the war. He fought from First Manassas and Shiloh (where he suffered his first wound of the war) through all the campaigns and engagements of the Army of Tennessee: Perryville, Murfreesboro, Chickamauga, Missionary Ridge, Ringgold Gap, New Hope Church, Atlanta, Franklin, and Nashville. Yet his accounts of battles reflect his own limited perspective on the field. He frequently refers to individuals—his

1. To William Rose Benét, [20] March 1927, in Charles A. Fenton, ed., *Selected Letters of Stephen Vincent Benét* (New Haven: Yale University Press, 1960), 136.

friends—whose names, like his own, do not remind us of heroic deeds; people who, save in the loving memories of their families, have long since been buried in the sands of time. His commentary is valuable because it lacks pretension and offers us an unapologetic view of war from the ranks. There are fuller, longer accounts of the war, but few are so honest or direct. Bevens conveys to us the tedium of army life. He shows us that armies spent far more time marching from place to place, establishing camps, foraging, drilling, standing guard, coping with the weather, raising hell, and trying to pass the time than they did shooting at the enemy.

He tells us about what mattered to him, a common foot soldier. He joined the army and fought the Yankees because he was young, it was springtime, and his homeland was about to be invaded by a wicked foe. Like any good private, he likes to second-guess the tactics and strategies of his superiors, and he never hesitates to express his prejudices. He worshiped Albert Sidney Johnston and Joseph E. Johnston; he admired Patrick R. Cleburne; he was terrified of Nathan Bedford Forrest; and he doubted the ability of John Bell Hood. He did not care much for Negroes, particularly not for those blacks who fought in the Union army. While he and his immediate family were not slave owners, Bevens believed that blacks should occupy a subordinate position in society. Like most Confederate soldiers, he regarded the presence of blacks on the battlefield as an affront to honor. On the other hand, he did not consider that he was fighting a war to preserve slavery. He was not moved one way or another by that issue, and he certainly did not see himself as a poor man in a rich.man's fight.

Bevens's reminiscences are also valuable because they were written by an Arkansas soldier, a rare enough item among published chronicles of the war. Elihu C. Beckham, a sergeant in Company K, Twenty-first Arkansas Infantry, may have been the first Arkansan to recount his wartime experiences. He wrote a series of articles for an Izard County newspaper in 1887. Ten years later, Joe Scott, of Washington County, published a slender pamphlet telling his story about service in several Confederate army units. A few veterans then published their recollections in the *Confederate Veteran* and a few Arkansas newspapers in the early twentieth century. William E. Woodruff, Jr., postwar editor of the *Arkansas Gazette,* published his military experiences in 1903. The ladies had also become active by that time, as the United Confederate Veterans of Arkansas published a collection of reminiscences by the state's Confederate women in 1907.[2]

As welcome as these initial memoirs may have been, their usefulness was hampered by three things. First, most of them were only a few pages long, and they had been written with little concern for detail or accuracy. Second, most early accounts, particularly the ones in the *Confederate Veteran* and in the women's anthology, focused on isolated incidents. Few people sought to convey the entirety of their wartime experiences. Third, all of the longer and more valuable accounts had been printed in obscurity and produced in limited quantities. They gained little attention outside of their immediate communities, and few have survived in their original forms.

The situation has improved somewhat in recent years. The wartime correspondence, diaries, and recollections of many

2. Elihu C. Beckham, "Where I Was and What I Saw During the War," *Stream of History* 18 (November 1979-July 1981), 3–20, and (November 1981), 23–43; Joe M. Scott, *Four Years' Service in the Southern Army* (Mulberry, Ark.: Leader Office, 1897); William E. Woodruff, *With the Light Guns in '61–'65: Reminiscences of Eleven Arkansas, Missouri, and Texas Light Batteries in the Civil War* (Little Rock: Central Printing Office, 1903); United Confederate Veterans of Arkansas, ed., *Confederate Women of Arkansas in the Civil War 1861–'65: Memorial Reminiscences* (Little Rock; H.G. Pugh, 1907).

Arkansans have been rescued from the obscurity of attic trunks and public archives to be preserved in print. The Arkansas Historical Association, through the pages of the *Arkansas Historical Quarterly,* has led the way in this effort to preserve the state's Civil War legacy, and many county historical societies deserve credit, too. Small but valuable county bulletins and magazines have published wartime accounts that otherwise would have been lost. Still, when it comes to reminiscences of the war, most efforts have been plagued by the old defects of brevity and, for those confined to county publications, obscurity. Moreover, even the more complete and readily available memoirs lack proper annotation. Obscure people remain obscure, muddled events remain muddled, and incorrect statements remain uncorrected. Thus, some otherwise good accounts of the war years never realize their potential value.[3]

William Bevens's reminiscences began in obscurity, too. He wrote and published his volume shortly before World War I. It was intended primarily for local distribution in Jackson County, having been printed at Newport, Arkansas, and paid for by the Lucien C. Gause Chapter No. 508, United Daughters of the Confederacy. It sold for one dollar per copy, and its principal purpose was to raise money for the erection of a monument to the Jackson Guards, Bevens's old unit, which became Company G, First Arkansas Infantry. The monument, a handsome granite obelisk, was erected and dedicated on November 25, 1914, on the courthouse lawn at Newport, four miles south of Jacksonport. It was later moved to Jacksonport and now stands near the old

3. The best general guide to published firsthand accounts of the war by Arkansans is Tom W. Dillard and Michael Dougan, compls., *Arkansas History: A Selected Research Bibliography* (Little Rock: Department of Arkansas Natural and Cultural Heritage, 1984).

Jacksonport courthouse on the grounds of the Jacksonport State Park.[4]

The Jackson County Historical Society twice tried to resurrect interest in Bevens's book and to make it more readily available. By 1970, only a few scattered copies of the original volume had survived. So the society reproduced the reminiscences serially in its magazine, *Stream of History,* between July 1970 and April 1972.[5] In 1977, the society went a step further by reproducing a limited quantity of the reminiscences in pamphlet form. At first, this "pamphlet" was unbound, but in 1984 the society secured the wherewithal to bind the pages in an attractive hardcover edition and attach an index to persons' names. Unfortunately, neither the serial republication nor the pamphlet included annotation or explanatory notes for Bevens's text.[6]

This new edition of the Bevens book is based on the original 1914 text. As editor, I have largely restricted myself to filling gaps left by Bevens. When possible, I have buttressed Bevens's view of events by referring to letters, diaries, and other reminiscences that describe the same episodes. The original text has been altered only in minor ways. First, all obvious typographical errors have been corrected. Second, Bevens's misspellings of the names of persons and places have been corrected. Third, a few dates, enclosed in

4. William E. Bevens, *Reminiscences of a Private, Company "G," First Arkansas Regiment Infantry, May, 1861 to 1865* (Newport, Ark.: Lucien C. Gause Chapter No. 508, UDC, 1914); *Confederate Veteran* 23 (February 1915), 88; Marjorie May McDonald, et al., *Souvenir Program presenting Glimpses and Highlights of the 135 Years of Jackson County History* (Newport, Ark.: Jackson County Historical Society, 1965).

5. *Stream of History* 8 (July 1970), 45–52, (October 1970), 35–40; 9 (January 1971), 13–26, (April 1971), 33–40, (July 1971), 33–39, (October 1971), 29–39; 10 (January 1972), 23–39, (April 1972), 25–40.

6. William E. Bevens, *Reminiscences of a Private, Company "G," First Arkansas Regiment Infantry, May, 1861 to 1865* (Newport, Ark.: Jackson County Historical Society, 1977).

brackets, have been added for the sake of clarity. Fourth, Bevens's version of the Company G roster, which he had apparently compiled from memory, has been altered to reflect surviving records in the National Archives. Fifth, for the convenience of readers, the text has been divided into three chapters. The original text was published as a continuous narrative. I have begun chapter 2 on what was page 26 of the original text, and chapter 3 on what was page 56. The photographic portraits all appeared in the original volume, but the maps tracing Bevens's path through the war have been added, as have four illustrations of places mentioned in his narrative. The only portion of the original text to be deleted is four pages of material relating to postwar meetings of the company's surviving members. The notes, while supplemental, should be read as an integral part of the text. Bevens leaves many gaps in his story. The notes are intended to fill those gaps, correct errors, and supply neglected details.

We have little to indicate what sources Bevens used in writing his memoirs. He presumably talked to other surviving members of his company. Casualty figures, dates, and similar details could have been obtained from *Century Magazine*'s "Battles and Leaders of the Civil War" series, published during the 1880s, as well as from *The War of the Rebellion: A Compilation of the Official Records of the Union and Confederate Armies,* published between 1880 and 1900. He seems also to have gleaned some information from the *Confederate Veteran,* first published in 1893. Evidence that Bevens contacted other veterans or their families is found in a memorandum book he kept at the time he was writing his manuscript, around 1913–14. The memorandum book contains the names and addresses of former comrades or their wives as well as scattered notes that pertain to battles and episodes connected with the war.

The only known reference used by Bevens to jog his memory

was a "diary" kept by a fellow member of Company G, Thomas R. Stone. The Stone document, which exists only in manuscript, may have started out as a genuine diary, or perhaps it was based on a diary, brief and sketchy at best, that Stone kept during the war. However, somewhere along the line he fleshed it out so that it, too, is really a memoir. Too many of Stone's comments betray a prior knowledge of events or refer to events in the past tense for it to be a genuine diary. The Stone document covers a relatively brief period of time. It begins with the mustering in of the Jackson Guards and the company's departure for Virginia, in May 1861. Stone then leaves large gaps between July and October 1861 and between November 1861 and March 1862. The "diary" ends abruptly in July 1862, when Stone transferred to another regiment. Yet Bevens clearly used the document. The wording of passages in his own reminiscences are quite similar to passages in Stone, and the only surviving copy of Stone's manuscript is a copy transcribed by Bevens in April 1911. It has been preserved in the collections of the Arkansas History Commission, Little Rock.

The Man

William Edwin Bevens stood 5'6" and had gray eyes, light hair, and a fair complexion. He was not a native Arkansan. His father, Dr. Alfred Bevens, hailed from Charleston, South Carolina, and did not settle his family at Batesville, Independence County, Arkansas, until 1843. Along the way, Dr. Bevens had stopped off at Morgantown, Morgan County, North Carolina, where he married Jane Louise McGuire, and where four of their six children were born. William was born there on March 5, 1841, as were his older brother, Elam, and two sisters, Sarah and Emma. Mary and

Thomas Alfred would be born at Batesville. William's family was one of several contingents of Bevenses and McGuires who emigrated to Independence County during the 1840s. Most prominent was an uncle, Judge William C. Bevens, who served on the circuit court and represented Batesville in the Arkansas legislature during the 1850s.[7]

William received his formal education at the Soulesbury Institute in Batesville and from a tutor, Ralph R. Kellogg. Kellogg, a native of Pennsylvania, also happened to be William's brother-in-law, having married Sarah in December 1850 when he was twenty-seven and she was seventeen. Kellogg also served as the county's circuit court clerk between 1848 and 1854. William moved to Jacksonport, Jackson County, about 1856 to clerk in his brother Elam's newly opened pharmacy on Adams Street. He was working there and learning the pharmacy trade when the war began. William boarded for at least part of that period with Kellogg, his sister, and three nieces, all of whom had also moved to Jacksonport. Kellogg served as Jackson County's circuit court

7. James Logan Morgan, trans., *Independence County, Arkansas, Seventh Census Free Population Schedules 1850* (Newport, Ark.: Northeast Arkansas Genealogical Association, 1971), 43, 58, 60; and *Genealogical Records of Independence County, Arkansas, 1845–1850* (Newport, Ark.: Northeast Arkansas Genealogical Association, 1972), 9; *Biographical and Historical Memoirs of Northeast Arkansas* (Chicago: Goodspeed Publishing Company, 1889), 644, 690; Robert Neill, "Reminiscences of Independence County," *Publications of Arkansas Historical Association* 3 (1911), 345; *Confederate Veteran* 33 (April 1925), 149; Compiled Service Records of Confederate Soldiers Who Served in Organizations from the State of Arkansas, National Archives Microcopy No. 317, Roll 46. Some sources maintain that Bevens was born on May 5. See "Biographical Memoranda of Confederate Veterans of Jackson County, Arkansas, 1912," *Stream of History* 12 (July 1974), 17–18. For a sketch of Bevens's younger brother, Thomas Alfred Bevens, who was also a Confederate veteran, see *Confederate Veteran* 27 (August 1919), 306.

clerk from 1858 to 1868. When the war started, he owned more than twelve thousand dollars in real and personal property. Elam left the pharmacy in Kellogg's care when he entered the army in August 1862. That obligation lasted only until November 1863, when, recalled William, "The Yanks came and destroyed everything—even smashed the bottles and rolled the barrels into the river." With the business thus "swept away," Kellogg, who had been serving on the county's Vigilance Committee and Purchasing Committee, enlisted in the army.[8]

After the war, in September 1865, Bevens opened his own drugstore in Jacksonport. "I opened with a small stock of drugs on one side of a one room store," he recalled, "L. L. Moore doing business on the other side. He had been the head of that great firm L. L. Moore & Co., and now broke, like the rest of us, was starting a small grocery store, doing all the work himself." Both men slept in the half story above the store, and Bevens again took meals at his sister's home. His fortunes, however, soon changed for the better. In 1867, he married the comely Virginia Green who, in time, bore two sons, Edwin and Joe L. Bevens. William's business prospered to the point that he could afford to build a two-room store, rent out one-half, and establish his pharmacy in the other

8. Morgan, trans., *Independence County, Arkansas, Seventh Census*, 59, 61; *Biographical and Historical Memoirs*, 622, 833; "Biographical Memoranda of Confederate Veterans," 17–18; *Confederate Veteran* 33 (April 1925), 149; Lady Elizabeth Watson, *Fight and Survive!* (Conway, Ark.: River Road Press, 1974), 14–15, 77–78, 165; Mabel West, "Jacksonport, Arkansas; Its Rise and Decline," *Arkansas Historical Quarterly* 9 (Winter 1950), 243; Population Schedules [Free] of the Eighth United States Census, 1860, Arkansas, National Archives Microcopy No. 653, Roll 44, pp. 654, 662; William E. Bevens, "Makers of Jackson County; Short Stories of Early Pioneers, and Something about the Founding of Old Jacksonport," eds., Lady Elizabeth Luker and James Logan Morgan, *Stream of History* 20 (March 1984), 23–27. The last-mentioned source is the edited version of a pamphlet of the same title published by Bevens in 1923. The edited version is used here because of its greater accuracy.

half. Then, in his own words, Bevens "began to hustle." Soon, he had built his own home and a new store. However, things soured in 1873, when the newly constructed Cairo & Fulton Railroad by-passed Jacksonport. The railroad ruined Jacksonport, which had flourished because of the trade along the White River. Most of the town's citizens gradually moved "bag and baggage" to Newport, which soon became the county seat. Bevens, rather than following the crowd, returned with his family to Batesville.[9]

Bevens opened a new drugstore in Batesville. It was located on lower Main Street, just below Laman's Wholesale Grocery Store. The town already had two druggists, including Eugene R. Goodwin, who, having opened business in 1846, operated the oldest drugstore in the state. All three men engaged in spirited advertising campaigns, and Bevens seems to have attracted his share of customers. Bevens prospered in Batesville. He purchased a magnificent house at 715 East Main, invested in Batesville real estate, became active in the Democratic party, labored as a steward in the Methodist Episcopal Church, served on the city council during the mid-1880s, served as county clerk for two years (1890–92), and saw his sons grow up and graduate from Arkansas College (founded at Batesville in 1872). Bevens even ran for mayor of Batesville in 1886 against John W. McDowell. When the election ended in a tie, the incumbent mayor, J. M. Bartlett, retained his office.[10]

9. Bevens, "Makers of Jackson County," 26–27; James Logan Morgan, ed., *Centennial History of Newport, Arkansas, 1875–1975* (Newport, Ark.: Jackson County Historical Society, 1975), 5–8, 23; West, "Jacksonport, Arkansas," 252–58.

10. Linda Fulbright, "When Hairdressers Made Housecalls," *Independence County Chronicle* 13 (October 1971), 37; Clyde Stewart, compl., "Independence County Officials 1820–1966," *Independence County Chronicle* 8 (January 1977), 13; John Q. Wolf, "My Fifty Years in Batesville, Arkansas," eds. Nancy Britton and Nana Farris, *Independence County Chronicle* 23 (October 1981–January 1982), 7–8, 18.

Despite his contentment, the ties to his old Jacksonport-Newport friends became too strong for Bevens, so he moved his family to Newport about 1897. Once there, with time and his life marching rapidly onward, he began to think more often about the past, about the war. This is not to say he had earlier forgotten about the war. In fact, as early as 1877, before leaving Jacksonport, Bevens and five other members of the old Jackson Guards had met to organize a reunion dinner. Fifteen members attended the festivities, held on May 4, 1877, and a dozen other men responded that circumstances prohibited them from attending. This total of twenty-seven men represented all known survivors of the Guards. Those at the dinner resolved to form a permanent organization that would meet every year thereafter on May 5, the anniversary of their first muster in 1861. How faithfully they kept their resolution after Jacksonport began to break up is unclear, but in the early 1890s Confederate veterans throughout Jackson County formed a camp of the United Confederate Veterans. They congregated every September between 1893 and 1900 at "Camp Cleburne" on the banks of the White River, midway between Newport and Jacksonport. The high point of their week-long festivities was a sham battle in which the "wounded" were bandaged with dressings that had been stained with red dye. A photograph of the 1899 encampment shows over a hundred men present.[11]

It is unclear whether Bevens participated in the White River reunions while living in Batesville. However, once in Newport, he threw himself into Confederate veterans activities. He joined Tom Hindman Camp No. 318, United Confederate Veterans, and served as camp adjutant. He published several short pieces, mostly biographical sketches of departed comrades, in the *Confederate*

11. Bevens, *Reminiscences of a Private*, 82–85; McDonald, et al., Souvenir Program, 44.

Veteran. He became "a moving spirit" in the erection of the Confederate monument at Newport, and he wrote his wartime reminiscences to help defray its cost. The base of the obelisk bore the names of his old comrades in the Jackson Guards, and every year on the anniversary of its dedication he reverently placed a commemorative wreath before the monument. Writing his reminiscences inspired Bevens to probe the past more broadly, the result being an anecdotal history of Jackson County, published in 1923. That was just a year before his death, which came on August 5, 1924. Bevens had remained active until the end. He worked daily at his drugstore, having been joined in the business by his younger son, Joe. Following funeral services at Newport's First Methodist Church, Bevens was buried in Batesville. He was the last survivor of old Company G.[12]

The Times

From the days of Andrew Jackson, Arkansans had voted Democratic. In the three decades before the Civil War, this Democratic juggernaut had been directed by a few dominant Little Rock families. The entrenched power of this oligarchy was successfully challenged by Thomas C. Hindman in the late 1850s. Hindman's challenge, highlighted by the election of Henry M. Rector as governor in 1860, succeeded for several reasons. First, the upstarts had appealed to the social and economic divisions between non-planters and the old aristocrats in Little Rock. Second, they had

12. Bevens's contributions to the *Confederate Veteran* appear in 25 (January 1917), 34; 25 (April 1917), 134; 27 (August 1919), 306; 28 (February 1920), 70–71; 30 (February 1922), 48–49; 30 (April 1922), 149; 30 (August 1922), 308; 32 (March 1924), 106–07; 32 (April 1924), 145. For the Newport monument dedication ceremony see *Confederate Veteran*, 23 (February 1915), 88.

appealed, perhaps unwittingly, to new immigrants in the state, mostly from Tennessee, Kentucky, and the Carolinas. The newcomers felt no allegiance to the oligarchy and saw the solutions offered by Hindman's Democrats for solving the state's economic problems as sensible. Then, too, the Hindman challenge was aided by many Whigs, who saw the renegades as a means of ousting their old foes. Thus, on the eve of the Civil War, state political power was being contested by three factions: the oligarchy, Hindman Democrats, and a small yet vocal coalition of Whigs and Know-Nothings.[13]

However, the volatile issues that sparked the approaching presidential election of 1860 soon engulfed the state's internal struggle. On the rightness of slavery, the expansion of slavery into the territories, and the legality of secession, Arkansas Democrats, and therefore a majority of Arkansans, stood firmly with the South. The state's first step down the road of secession came during the presidential campaign. As the Democratic party spent much of the summer trying to hold a nominating convention, only one of Arkansas's eight delegates to the convention supported the "regular" party and its nominee, Stephen A. Douglas. Most Arkansas Democrats cheered the nomination of John C. Breckinridge by the southern Democratic party. Not to be outdone in the impending donnybrook, the state's Whigs and Know-Nothings flocked to the Constitutional Union party and its nominee, John Bell. It mattered little. Breckinridge won the state with 53 percent of the popular vote.

Abraham Lincoln, of course, won the national election, but the

13. The best accounts of the political background of secession in Arkansas, although they sometimes disagree with each other, are Michael B. Dougan, *Confederate Arkansas: The People and Policies of a Frontier State in Wartime* (University, Ala.: University of Alabama Press, 1976) and James M. Woods, *Rebellion and Realignment: Arkansas's Road to Secession* (Fayetteville: University of Arkansas Press, 1987). The following paragraphs are based on these two works.

reaction to his victory in Arkansas was not as shrill as it was in the Deep South. Lincoln had not won a single vote in Arkansas, yet few Arkansans spoke of following South Carolina out of the Union. There had never been very many fire-eaters in Arkansas, so, even though Lincoln and the Republicans did speak of restricting the expansion of slavery, their promise not to tamper with slavery where it already existed led Arkansans to wait on events.

That is not to say the state lacked rabble-rousers and immediate secessionists. Thomas Hindman, for one, and congressman-elect Edward W. Gantt (a Hindman ally), for another, spoke of joining the secession movement by late November. Some members of the old oligarchy, too, like Senator Robert W. Johnson, encouraged secession, and, by mid-December, Governor Rector had announced that if Mississippi and Louisiana seceded, Arkansas's economic future must necessarily be linked to the new southern Confederacy.

However, the attitudes of nonpoliticians were more often shaped by geography than by party affiliation. Generally, the hills of northern and western Arkansas bred Unionists while the lowlands of the state's southern regions and the Delta of eastern Arkansas heard the fiery rhetoric of secession. The hills had been populated by non-slaveholding farmers and herders from the upper South, especially Missouri, Kentucky, and Tennessee. Lowlanders more often depended on slave labor and high cotton prices for their financial health. Still, the state as a whole resisted the secessionist impulse. Only with the Confederacy an established fact did Arkansas vote (on February 18, 1861, the same day Jefferson Davis was inaugurated as Confederate president) to approve the convening of a state convention to debate the merits of secession. Even then, Unionist delegates held a majority of the convention's seats.

By April, the situation outside Arkansas had changed. Lincoln's call to arms following the surrender of Fort Sumter pushed most Arkansans toward the Confederate cause. Even so, the step had been a reluctant one. Only when southern equality seemed unlikely under a Republican national government did most people sever their ties to the Union. In this they typified the upper South. "While Arkansas is not committed to the doctrine of secession," read the secession manifesto, "she is against the coercion by the Federal government of any seceded State." Not everyone agreed, and some holdouts, especially in the northwestern part of the state, would persist in their opposition to the Confederacy. More impressive, however, were the hundreds of young men who rushed to don Confederate uniforms. Even in the Ozarks, Union aggression changed many attitudes. Senator Johnson happened to be addressing a jeering Unionist crowd at Bentonville when news arrived of Lincoln's call for troops. "All was changed in an instant," reported one gentleman. "What! Call upon the southern people to shoot down their neighbors, help those from whom we have for years only received injury and wrong . . . No, never!"[14]

Governor Rector acted even before an ordinance of secession was officially approved. As early as February 8, he had ordered the seizure of the Federal arsenal at Little Rock and evacuation of approximately seventy-five Federal troops stationed there. When events at Fort Sumter promised inevitable membership by his state in the Confederacy, he mobilized the Arkansas militia and ordered it to capture the Federal garrison at Fort Smith. By the time the militia arrived, on April 23, the Federals there, the last U.S. troops within the state, had long since moved to Kansas. When news arrived a few days later that Virginia had seceded, die-hard Unionists agreed to reconvene the secession convention, which

14. Quotes are from Woods, *Rebellion and Realignment*, 149, 155.

had been recessed, and vote on the issue of secession. When the vote came, on May 6, only five of seventy delegates dared to vote against it.

Jackson County reflected all the ambiguity, anxiety, and confusion that prevailed in the state during the early months of 1861. Located in the eastern half of the state, Jackson County rested on the fringe of the Delta. In terms of wealth, Jackson rested in a middle tier of counties, neither as prosperous as the state's wealthiest counties nor as poor as the poorest ones. It was a prosperous farming community with rich bottom lands fed by the White, Black, and Cache rivers, Village Creek, and Bayou Deview. Jackson County's slave population had increased by nearly 6 percent between 1850 and 1860, but the white population had grown by 216 percent, one of the fastest rates of growth in the state. Thus the white population of 7,957 depended but little on the black population of 2,535. Voters had rallied overwhelmingly to neither Breckinridge nor Bell during the presidential election. Still, when the issue of union or disunion had to be faced, Jackson County voted for disunion.[15]

The young men of Jackson County, many of whom had been born outside the state, rushed to enlist in Confederate service. Eleven companies of infantry and cavalry, plus a battery of artillery, were raised in the county, about twelve hundred men in all. Among the first units to be formed was the Jackson Guards, organized at Jacksonport on May 5, 1861, that soon became Company G of the First Arkansas Infantry Regiment. Another Confederate infantry unit claimed the title of the First Arkansas, but it was a pretender to that lofty title. Early in the war, Patrick Cleburne commanded a unit known variously as the First Infantry

15. *Ibid.* 171, 186–87, 190–91; *Biographical and Historical Memoirs,* 832–39.

Regiment of State Troops and the First Infantry Regiment of Arkansas Volunteers, but this regiment was finally designated the Fifteenth Arkansas.[16]

William Bevens, caught up in the whirl of activity, could not resist the prospect of participating in a glorious war for southern independence. He enlisted in the Jackson Guards for ninety days, as long as most people thought it would take to beat the Yankees. He remained in Confederate service for fifteen hundred days. What follows is his recollection of those eventful days as lived by himself and his comrades.

Before Bevens tells his story, I wish to thank those people who aided me in preparing his reminiscences for publication. John Griffin of Searcy, Arkansas, initiated the project by bringing the Bevens volume to the attention of the University of Arkansas Press. Miller Williams, director of the press, deserves credit for recognizing the merits of the Bevens book, and Dr. Willard B. Gatewood, Jr., Distinguished Professor in the department of history, University of Arkansas, confirmed Williams' initial enthusiasm and suggested me as a likely editor.

As I sought to compile and verify information about Bevens, Company G, and the First Arkansas Infantry, I received assistance and encouragement from several energetic and enthusiastic people. I am particularly grateful to Dr. Nancy S. Griffith of the Regional Studies Center, Arkansas College; Mrs. Lady Elizabeth Luker, of Newport, Arkansas; Rebecca A. Rose and Malinda W. Collier, of the Museum of the Confederacy, Richmond, Virginia; William

16. John C. Hammock, *With Honor Untarnished: The Story of the First Arkansas Infantry Regiment, Confederate States Army* (Little Rock: Pioneer Press, 1961), 13; Howell and Elizabeth Purdue, *Pat Cleburne, Confederate General* (Hillsboro, Tex.: Hill Junior College Press, 1973), 79, 97.

Long, of the Old State House, Little Rock; and the staffs of the Special Collections, Mullins Library, University of Arkansas, Fayetteville; the Arkansas History Commission, Little Rock; and the Newport Public Library, Newport, Arkansas.

Finally, I think back to Stephen Vincent Benét and his efforts to comprehend America's Civil War. As he worked diligently on the manuscript of *John Brown's Body,* Benét checked and rechecked his facts, investigated and tried to document the most minute events in his story. As he neared completion of his task, Benét let slip an exasperated remark that has flashed through the mind of many a writer, and which certainly summarizes my own thoughts: "These little things are hell to check on and I have had a lot of grief trying to do so. As it is, I will probably be hopped on by various and sundry when the book comes out. But I want to be as accurate as possible wherever I can."[17]

17. To John Farrar, [27] April 1928, in Fenton, ed., *Selected Letters,* 160.

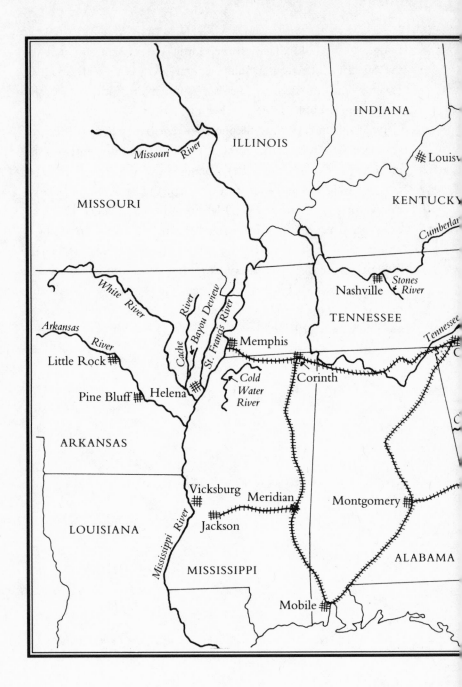

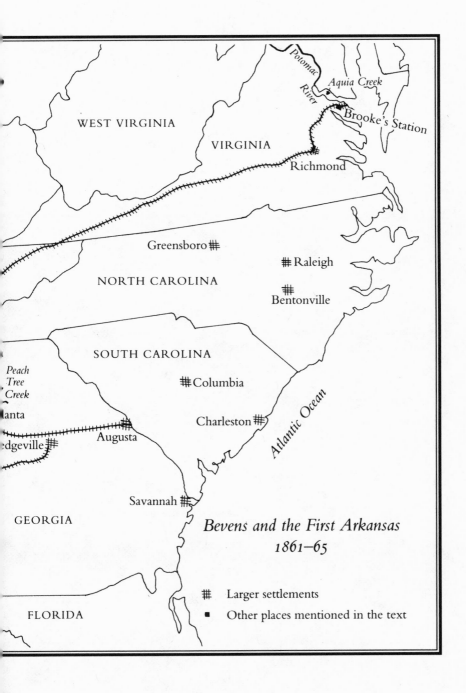

WEST VIRGINIA

VIRGINIA

Potomac River

Aquia Creek

Brooke's Station

Richmond

Greensboro ⌗

⌗ Raleigh

NORTH CAROLINA

⌗
Bentonville

SOUTH CAROLINA

Peach
Tree
Creek

⌗ Columbia

Atlantic Ocean

anta

Charleston ⌗

⌗ Augusta

dgeville ⌗

Savannah ⌗

GEORGIA

*Bevens and the First Arkansas
1861–65*

⌗   Larger settlements
■   Other places mentioned in the text

FLORIDA

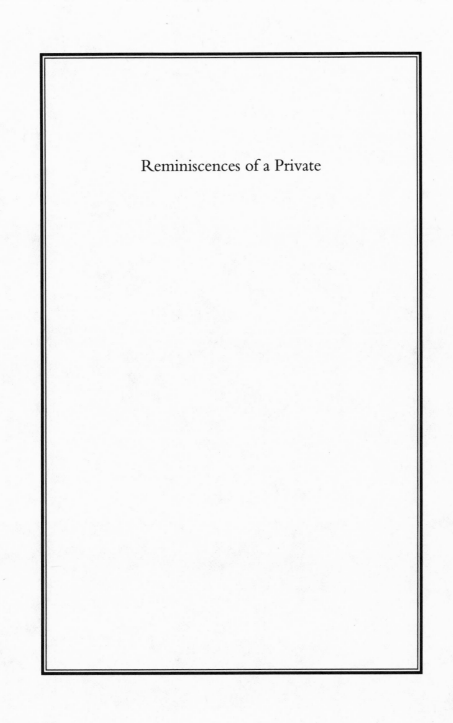

Reminiscences of a Private

Chapter One

WHEN our children come from other states and from foreign lands to visit Jacksonport, the old home of their parents, they find the pitiful remnant of a village. Streets overgrown with weeds, dilapidated wooden cottages, a tumbled down brick court house, meet their eyes. One or two well kept homes and a prosperous general store only emphasize the prevailing air of decay. The visitors may walk a mile down the road to the old town Elizabeth, and find no trace of habitation. The persimmon, the paw paw and the muscadine flourish in spaces that were once busy streets. When they remember that this place lacked only one vote of being made the capital of the state they may ponder on the uncertainty of human destiny.

1. Jacksonport became the county seat of Jackson County (created in 1829, seven years before Arkansas became a state) in 1854. It remained so until 1892. The town, settled originally in the 1830s, became a major northeast Arkansas river port in the 1850s. *Biographical and Historical Memoirs of Northeast Arkansas* (Chicago: Goodspeed Publishing Company, 1889), 832–39; Lady Elizabeth Watson, *Fight and Survive!* (Conway, Ark.: River Road Press, 1974), 1–2; Mabel West, "Jacksonport, Arkansas; Its Rise and Decline," *Arkansas Historical Quarterly* 9 (Winter 1950), 231–42.

But in 1861 Jacksonport was an important town. It was the county seat when Jackson county was much larger than it is now. Woodruff was a part of it and the whole formed a wealthy section of the state, the rich "bottoms" producing the finest cotton. Jacksonport was situated where Black River flows into White River, and was the center of distribution for many counties. At low water, which was the greater part of the year, it was at the head of navigation and people came from fifty miles to trade there, hauling overland all freight for Batesville and upper points.

It was then one of the great river towns, and one of the most fascinating occupations of my boyhood was watching the steamboats. We had two mail steamers, side-wheelers, up-to-date, with all kinds of accommodations for passengers and freight, and I have seen nine steamers loading and unloading at once. One packet from Louisville, one from St. Louis, two from Memphis, two from Upper Black River, and two from New Orleans. I have seen one of the last, "The Seminole," with a load of fifteen hundred bales of cotton.[1]

At that time Jacksonport had a population of twenty-five hundred. The surrounding farms and plantations, cultivated by negro slaves, were owned by the Tunstalls, Waddills, Robinsons, Gardners and

2. According to the census of 1860, Jackson County's population included 7,957 whites, 2,535 slaves, and 1 free black.

3. Alexander Corbin Pickett, born about 1826 in Virginia to Steptoe and Sarah O. (Chilton) Pickett, was a lawyer and veteran of the Mexican War. He organized the Guards originally as a volunteer infantry company of the Thirty-fourth Arkansas Militia in early 1860. He later became the colonel of the Tenth Missouri Infantry.

4. According to its original muster roll, the company numbered 111 officers and men. This roll is provided in John C. Hammock, *With Honor Untarnished: The Story of the First Arkansas Infantry Regiment, Confederate States Army* (Little Rock: Pioneer Press, 1961), 152–54. The roster provided by Bevens in *Reminiscences of a Private, Company "G," First Arkansas Regiment Infantry, May, 1861 to 1865* (Newport, Ark.: Lucien C. Gause Chapter No. 508, UDC, 1914), 85–89, lists 155 officers and men, and elsewhere he describes the composition of the company as being "one hundred and fifty-six strong, made up of lawyers, merchants, doctors, clerks, mechanics, farmers, schoolboys—the best that the days could offer." See William E. Bevens, "Makers of Jackson County: Short Stories of Early Pioneers, and Something about the Founding of Old Jacksonport," ed. by Lady Elizabeth Luker and James Logan Morgan, *Stream of History* 21

(March 1984), 26. Bevens originally published this brief history of Jackson County and Jacksonport at Newport, Arkansas, about 1923. The Luker and Morgan edition, published in two parts in *Stream of History* (December 1983 and March 1984), corrects errors made by Bevens and so is cited here instead of the original volume. The most complete roster of the company is in Watson, *Fight and Survive!,* 153–55, which identifies 166 officers and men. Of these, 143 have been identified from surviving service records; the other 23 are men listed by Bevens, but their service records have not survived. The roster provided in the Appendix of this book is drawn from the 143 surviving records in Compiled Service Records of Confederate Soldiers Who Served in Organizations from the State of Arkansas, National Archives Microcopy 317, Rolls 46–52 (cited hereafter as Service Records). Based on these records, the known occupations of 100 men in Company G bear out Bevens's characterization of them. They included 42 farmers, 14 clerks, 7 laborers, 5 carpenters, 5 merchants, 4 lawyers, 3 saddlers, 2 overseers, 2 painters, 2 cooks, and 1 mechanic, journalist, druggist, river pilot, doctor, hosteler, soldier, tanner, steward, cooper, mason, printer, grocer, shoemaker, plasterer, and surveyor.

5. Mrs. Robinson was the wife of John Robinson, whose family had been among the county's original settlers. He served as county judge from

others. Old fashioned Southern hospitality prevailed in town and country, and we who were fortunate enough to live there "Befo de wah" think no other can ever equal it, no other town can ever boast of such beautiful girls, such handsome boys, such noble women, such brilliant men.[2]

When the war cry sounded Captain A. C. Pickett, a fine lawyer and an old Mexican War veteran, made up our company, and called it the "Jackson Guards."[3] This company to the number of one hundred and twenty was formed of the best boys in the county. Sons of plantation-owners, lawyers, doctors, druggists, merchants,—the whole South rose as one man, to defend its rights. The young men, many of us barely twenty years of age, knew nothing of war. We thought we could take our trunks and dress suits. We besieged Capt. Pickett and nearly drove him to distraction with questions as to how many suits we should take. He nearly paralyzed us by telling us to leave behind all fancy clothes, and to take only one suit, a woolen top shirt and two suits of underwear.[4]

The noble women of Jacksonport made our flag. The wife of Judge Robinson bought the silk in Memphis. Mrs. Densford made the stars and all the ladies, old and young, worked on it, for love of those who were to bear it in battle.[5]

On the Fifth of May, 1861 we were ready. It was a

1844 to 1850. Mrs. Densford is probably Mary Densford, the twenty-seven-
year-old wife of William B. Densford,
a Kentucky-born engineer, who
would serve as a sergeant in Company
G. See note 15 below. Bevens elsewhere describes the banner as "an
exquisite silk flag, embroidered by the
women of Jacksonport." Bevens,

"Makers of Jackson County," 25. The
flag, which would, in due course,
become the regimental flag of the
First Arkansas Infantry, was donated
many years after the war to the
Museum of the Confederacy in
Richmond, Virginia. See note 23
below.

W. E. Bevens

1861

6. Elsewhere, Bevens calls Mary Thomas Caldwell, daughter of Judge Caldwell, "one of the most popular girls who ever lived in Jacksonport." According to the census of 1860, she lived with the family of J. L. Watson, a Kentucky-born merchant worth over thirteen thousand dollars. She married Capt. John Calvin Matthews in 1863 at age twenty-one, and had several stirring adventures during the war. See Bevens, "Makers of Jackson County," 25–26; Sallie Walker Stockard, *The History of Lawrence, Jackson, Independence and Stone Counties of the Third Judicial District of Arkansas* (Little Rock: Arkansas Democrat, 1904), 72. Fannie E. Board was the seventeen-year-old daughter of Christopher W. Board, a merchant who served as colonel of the Thirty-fourth Regiment of Arkansas Militia. She had been born in Kentucky, as had her widowed father and one of her two sisters. She married Robert D. Bond, a private in Company G, in 1865. Pauline Hudson was a sixteen-year-old native of South Carolina who lived with her mother, Mary, a boardinghouse keeper. Pauline Hudson married Richard M. Davis (later the mayor of Newport, Arkansas) in 1863. One of the "others" who presented the flag was Mary Dillard, fifteen-year-old daughter of A. W. and Elizabeth Dillard. Mr. Dillard, a farmer, was a native of North Carolina who moved first to Missouri and then to Arkansas, where he owned land worth nine thousand dollars in 1860. His wife and all but the youngest of his six children had been born in Missouri.

7. Miss Caldwell's brief address and Sydney S. Gause's equally brief reply appeared in the *Jacksonport Herald* and are reprinted in Watson, *Fight and Survive!,* 4. Sydney S. Gause was a twenty-one-year-old lawyer and the brother of Lucien C. Gause, who was elected first lieutenant of the company and later became colonel of the Thirty-second Arkansas Infantry. Service Records, Roll 47.

8. Mary Patterson was the wife of James H. Patterson, a member of Arkansas's secession convention. In July he organized the Independent Jackson Rangers, which served in Col. John A. Schnable's Confederate Battalion of Missouri Cavalry.

gloomy day. The rain poured in torrents, but our company formed and marched to the Presbyterian church where the flag was to be presented. Every living soul in town was there, streets, yard and church overflowed with people, notwithstanding the rain. We had seats reserved for us, and felt very grand as we watched the young ladies on the platform. We thought they were the sweetest girls living, and the most beautiful. Misses Mary Thomas Caldwell, Fannie Board, Pauline Hudson, and others were there.[6] Miss Caldwell presented the colors with a short and touching speech. Sydney S. Gause received it in the name of the company, replying beautifully.[7] There was not a dry eye in the throng. Mothers were there who saw their sons perhaps for the last time. Fathers bade adieu to noble boys whom they had brought up to manly deeds of honor. Sisters separated from brothers. Sweethearts gave farewell to those whom they would love unto death. Who would not be moved to tears? We marched to the boat, and on the bank we stopped to give a last embrace to mother, wife, sister, sweetheart. That spot was hallowed with the tears that dropped upon the ground.

The boat was the *Mary Patterson,* named for an Augusta lady, wife of one of our great lawyers.[8] Its owner, Captain Morgan Bateman, with great generosity, offered to take us to Memphis. He was a man

9. Morgan Magness Bateman (1827–70) was born in Williamson County, Tennessee, of Beniah and Sarah (Magness) Bateman. The family, which included seven children, settled in Independence County, Arkansas Territory, in 1829. Bateman became a registered steamboat pilot in 1852. He obtained financial backing to build the *Mary Patterson* at Grand Glaize, Arkansas, and the boat was enrolled for service at Memphis in April 1859. It was 125 feet long and nearly 24 feet wide; it displaced over 105 net tons. It was scuttled with two other boats on June 17, 1863, in White River south of Clarendon, Arkansas, to block passage of two Federal ironclad gunboats. Bateman became a recruiter in August. He raised two companies: Company K, Thirtieth Arkansas Infantry, and Company E, First Arkansas Cavalry. Elam F. Bevens became first lieutenant (and later captain) of Company K, while Morgan became the captain of Company E. Bateman's unit, which served under Col. Archibald S. Dobbin, became known as Bateman's Company of Partisan Rangers. In 1864, he transferred to Col. Thomas J. Morgan's Second Arkansas Cavalry. He resumed his career on the river after the war until his death at Memphis, where he is buried at Elmwood Cemetery. Duane Huddleston, "Morgan Magness Bateman was a Steamboatman," *Stream of History* 16 (January 1978), 3–31.

10. With the Jackson Guards aboard, Bateman sailed the *Mary Patterson* upriver a short distance before turning around to steam past the cheering throng of friends and relations that lined the shore. The soldiers crowded along the boat's rails to wave and shout in return. All the while, Ensign William M. Mathews stood atop the pilot house and waved the company's new flag. Huddleston, "Morgan Magness Bateman," 16.

11. The "near tragedy" involved a mysterious stranger who had recently arrived in Grand Glaize, about ten miles south of Jacksonport. The residents of Grand Glaize had decided the man was a Union spy. Shortly before the arrival of the *Mary Patterson,* they seized him, shaved half of his head and beard, and stuffed him in a crate they had constructed for him. The crate was hauled down to the river so that it might be placed aboard the *Mary Patterson* for shipment to Abraham Lincoln. That did not satisfy some people. An elderly woman wanted to drown him in the river, and some of the Jackson Guards wanted to hang him from the jack staff of the *Mary Patterson*. Captain Pickett intervened and had him brought aboard in his box. After the Jackson Guards debarked at Memphis, Bateman sailed on to Cairo, Illinois, where he released the prisoner. Apparently, this same man eventually joined the Third Missouri Cavalry and served with that Union unit when it occupied Jacksonport later in the war. See West, "Jacksonport, Arkansas," 248–49. A contemporary report of the incident appears in Thomas R. Stone Diary,

of commanding ability, or he could never have handled so many wild young men. He never received a cent for his liberality, but he did not care. (He afterwards came back and made up a company of his own, with the assistance of his brother who went with him.)[9]

When we were on board at last the boat pulled off from shore, amid waving handkerchiefs and shouts. "Good-bye, good-bye," and no one present ever forgot that day.[10]

We had with us an Italian Band which had come up from New Orleans and became stranded in Jacksonport. It was a great band and afforded us much pleasure until we got to Memphis.

At every town, landing and woodpile there was a crowd to cheer us. At Grand Glaize there happened a near-tragedy, which was averted by Captain Pickett and Captain Morgan Bateman.[11] When we reached Des Arc, from which place we expected to march overland to Little Rock, Captain Pickett received a telegram from the governor to send in by wire our votes for Colonel of the Regiment and then proceed to Memphis. By Captain Pickett's advice our company voted for Flournoy. The rest of the Regiment voted for Fagan, who was elected. Fagan ever afterward felt hard toward Captain Pickett.[12]

We arrived at Memphis Thursday, May 9th. We

4–5, Arkansas History Commission, Little Rock. Another account appears in Mrs. V. Y. Cook, "Farewell to Jacksonport Guards," in United Confederate Veterans of Arkansas, ed., *Confederate Women in Arkansas in the Civil War 1861–'65: Memorial Reminiscences* (Little Rock: H. G. Pugh Company, 1907), 67–68. Thomas Stone (pp. 5–6) reports a similar incident further down the river at Lake Bluff, Arkansas. The company heard about a Union sympathizer who, a few days previous, had shot at some local people "for some trivial offence." One of the Jackson Guards, "a real Arkansas rowdy," went to the man's house, dragged him out of bed, and was preparing to give him "a genteel ducking" in the river when Captain Pickett again spoiled the fun.

12. Thompson B. Flournoy had organized the First Arkansas Infantry when Gov. Henry Rector commissioned him to raise a regiment in April, even before the Arkansas secession convention had met. Flournoy, born about 1804 in Kentucky, lived with his wife and two daughters in Desha County. He was an immensely wealthy planter who, according to the census of 1860, owned $240,000 in real property and $133,596 in personal property. James Fleming Fagan (1828–93) was born in Clarke County, Kentucky, but moved to Arkansas with his family at age ten. He served as a lieutenant in Col. Archibald Yell's regiment during the Mexican War and afterwards served a term in the state legislature. He was

the captain of the Saline Guards, which would become Company E in the First Arkansas when the regimental election occurred. The election was politically charged, with the Little Rock *True Democrat* backing Flournoy and the *Arkansas Gazette* supporting Fagan. Fagan was the clear choice of the soldiers. Said one member of the regiment, "Colonel Fagan is much esteemed and admired by all for his gentlemanly and gallant bearing." However, all parties commended Flournoy on his gracious acceptance of defeat. Fagan would be promoted to brigadier general in 1862 and major general in 1864. See Hammock, *With Honor Untarnished,* 10–14; Ezra J. Warner, *Generals in Gray: Lives of the Confederate Commanders* (Baton Rouge: Louisiana State University Press, 1959), 85–86. The quote is from the *Arkansas Gazette,* 29 June 1861, 2. With the regiment now formally organized and christened the First Arkansas Regiment, the Jackson Guards and the nine other volunteer companies that formed the regiment lost their distinctive local titles and were designated by letters of the alphabet. Thus the Jackson Guards became Company G. As implied, Company G did not march the fifty miles from Des Arc to Little Rock. Instead, after downing "a few mint juleps" and enjoying the Italian band, it left at about 2 P.M. for Memphis. Thomas Stone records much joking and horseplay aboard the *Mary Patterson* for the remainder of the journey (pp. 7–8).

14

W. E. Bevens

1912

13. The fairgrounds were about a mile from Memphis. Many men, becoming bored with camp life during the four-day stopover, slipped into town whenever possible. Memphis, a thriving town of 22,623 (including 3,684 slaves), gained a reputation early in the war as a debauched place where weary soldiers could find pleasure. Stone Diary, 8–9.

The Second Tennessee Volunteer Infantry Regiment (also called the Fifth Confederate Infantry Regiment) was composed primarily of Irishmen from Memphis and was known as the "Irish Regiment." Later, from July 1863 to July 1864, it would be brigaded with the First Arkansas. Thomas A. Wittington, et al., *Tennessee in the Civil War: A Military History of Confederate and Union Units with Available Rosters of Personnel,* 2 vols. (Nashville: Civil War Centennial Commission, 1964), I, 174–76.

14. The reference to "pump-soled" boots implies thin-soled and rather insubstantial footgear. Perhaps Bevens was the sentry of whom Thomas Stone wrote (pp. 8–9): "At one time one of the Boys got the Counter sign and gave it to all the rest and nearly all of us went up town."

15. The following information is provided for the men listed here who are not mentioned again in the text: Lucien Coatsworth Gause (1836–80), whose photograph appears later in the text, was born in North Carolina. He was graduated from the University of Virginia and studied law at Cumberland University, in Tennessee, before starting a law practice at Jacksonport in 1859. Gause was "an eloquent speaker" and owned "an excellent library." In 1862, he became colonel of the Thirty-second Arkansas Infantry. After the war he resumed his law practice at Jacksonport and served briefly in the state legislature (1866) and in the U.S. Congress (1875–79). Bevens, "Makers of Jackson County," 24; *Biographical Directory of the American Congress, 1774–1971* (Washington: Government Printing Office, 1971), 991.

Lucius L. Moore was a thirty-year-old merchant at the time of his enlistment. There is no record of his service after December 1861, so he probably did not re-enlist. Service Records, Roll 50.

James Franklin Hunter (1833–80) was born in Tennessee and moved with his family to Arkansas in 1849. He married Sopronia Caroline Selvige in 1857. A brother, William H. Hunter (1839–73), enlisted as a private in Company G. James was reduced to private in November 1861 and transferred to the Second Arkansas Infantry Battalion in December 1861. He soon became that unit's sergeant major. Later, in September 1862, he was elected captain of Company K, Fifth Arkansas Infantry (later designated the Thirtieth Arkansas). He returned to Arkansas after the war and worked as a carpenter. Service Records, Roll 48; Helen Marie Laux, "James F. Hunter, marched to the Fair Grounds to await the arrival of the rest of the Regiment, and were put into the same quarters with an Irish Regiment from Tennessee.[13]

I was put on guard inside the Fair Grounds. It rained all night. I had on new pump-soled boots, and being by mistake, left on duty, these tight boots caused me considerable pain. When the sergeant asked me how long I had been on duty I answered "all night." He informed me that I should have been on guard only two hours. I thought it a part of the game to stay on all night. So much for being a soldier fool![14]

The next day we were organized and officers were elected for the twelve months. They were:

A. C. Pickett, Captain.
L. C. Gause, First Lieutenant.
L.L. Moore, Second Lieutenant.
George Paine, Third Lieutenant.
James Hunter, Orderly Sergeant.
William Densford, First Sergeant.
John R. Loftin, Second Sergeant.
Peter Bach, Third Sergeant.
Clay Lowe, Fourth Sergeant.
John M. Waddill, First Corporal.
Henry Clements, Second Corporal.
Sam Shoup, Third Corporal.
W. E. Bevens, Fourth Corporal.[15]

Soldier and Builder," *Stream of History* 15 (January 1977), 19–21.

George N. Paine was a thirty-year-old merchant at the time of his enlistment. There is no record of his service after May 1861, so he probably did not re-enlist. Service Records, Roll 50.

William B. Densford, a thirty-two-year-old engineer, served until taken ill in the autumn of 1862 at Ringgold, Georgia. Thereafter he seems to have spent the remainder of the war on sick furlough. Service Records, Roll 47.

Peter Bach enlisted at age twenty-three and was the company's original fourth sergeant. However, by September 1862, for unexplained reasons, he was reduced to private. He is listed as sick in the military hospital at Jackson, Mississippi, in June–August 1864. Bach, who was born in Arkansas, stood 5'11" and had gray eyes and light hair. Service Records, Roll 46.

Henry C. Clements, a nineteen-year-old clerk in 1861, was the company's original third corporal. He stood 5'4" and had hazel eyes, brown hair, and a fair complexion. By September 1862, Clements was promoted to second sergeant. He was captured near Jonesboro, Georgia, on September 1, 1864, but exchanged a few weeks later. Service Records, Roll 46.

Three Veterans of Company "G"

Right: John Cathey, W. E. Bevens, John R. Loftin, Sr.

16. The company departed from the Memphis railhead on May 12 at 3 P.M. with the remainder of the regiment, which had arrived there from Little Rock. The immediate destination was Lynchburg, not Richmond. The train departed at 6 P.M. in cool, rainy weather. The foul weather, which continued through the night, caused hardships because the men traveled in open cattle cars. Stone Diary, 10–11.

17. Robert H. Crockett was captain of the Crockett Rifles (Company H) from DeWitt County. He later became colonel of the Seventeenth Arkansas Infantry. This was not the only occasion on which Crockett was called on to speak to local crowds. See *Confederate Veteran* 2 (March 1894), 89.

18. John R. Fellows (1832–96) was born at Troy, New York, but moved with his parents to Arkansas while still a boy. He opposed secession, but quit his lucrative law practice at Camden, Arkansas, to join Company C, First Arkansas, as a private in February 1862. Standing 5'5" and possessed of brown hair, hazel eyes, and ruddy complexion, Fellows transferred to the staff of Brig. Gen. William N. R. Beall in Mississippi following the battle of Shiloh. He was commissioned a captain while serving under Beall. After the war, Fellows moved to New York City, where he enjoyed a prominent public career with the Democratic party, including a term in the U.S. Congress (1891–93). Service Records, Roll 47; Compiled Service Records of Confederate General and Staff Officers and Non-Regimental Enlisted Men, National Archives Microcopy No. 331, Roll 91 (cited hereafter as Officers' Service Records); *Biographical Directory of the American Congress,* 933–34; *New York Times,* 8 December 1896, 8.

When the captain took charge there were only two men in the company who knew anything about military tactics or could even keep step. We stayed in Memphis four days. On Sunday afternoon with our new banner proudly waving, we marched through Memphis to the depot of the Memphis and Charleston Railway, where we entrained for Richmond, Va. Along the line of march were thousands of people and at every station was shown such enthusiasm as was never before known in the South. Everyone came down to greet us. Old men and women, young girls, even the negroes. We were showered with bouquets.[16] We were delayed at different stations by the crowds. They came to see the Arkansas Troops, and to hear Captain Bob Crockett speak. He was a conspicuous character from the manner of his dress, and also a celebrity from being a grandson of old David Crockett, hence was often called on for a speech.[17] On one occasion, however, some of the soldiers asked several citizens to call for Private J. R. Fellows, one of the best orators in the South. He so far eclipsed Captain Crockett that the latter ever after took second place.[18]

We passed through Knoxville and Bristol, debatable territory because Etheridge Brownlow and Andy Johnson, Union men of great ability and influence, lived in these places. To say there were hot times in

19. Bevens must be referring to William Gannaway Brownlow (1805–77), a Unionist newspaper editor who would serve as governor of Tennessee and in the U.S. Senate during Reconstruction. Andrew Johnson (1808–75), future president of the United States, was representing Tennessee in the U.S. Senate when the war started. He refused to join his state in the Confederacy, and when Union armies gained control of Tennessee in 1862, Abraham Lincoln appointed him military governor. This whole region of east Tennessee through which the regiment traveled was strongly Unionist in its sympathies.

Bevens omits a large part of the itinerary between Memphis and Bristol. The Memphis and Charleston Railroad passed through a corner of northeastern Mississippi and across northern Alabama before swinging back up toward Chattanooga and Knoxville. Thomas Stone's diary records a stop at Huntsville, Alabama, where Captain Crockett spoke and where the men got off the train to eat dinner at the Huntsville House on May 13. They made another stop at Stevenson, Alabama, where a telling episode occurred. The troops again got out of the cattle cars to stretch their legs. One of the men bought some eggs and borrowed a silver fork from a citizen with which to eat them. When he had finished his meal, he decided to keep the fork, and when the disgruntled owner protested, the soldier told him to charge the expense to Jefferson Davis. "After this," wrote Stone, "when the Boys wanted anything they would say charge it to Jeff Davis." Stone Diary, 11–12.

At Stevenson, the regiment switched to the cars of the Nashville and Chattanooga Railroad and arrived at Chattanooga on the morning of May 14. Stone found it "a dull and sultry place." The Second Tennessee Infantry joined them as they again switched railways, and they proceeded to Knoxville on the cars of the East Tennessee and Georgia Railroad. At Knoxville, the regiment suffered its first casualty when a fellow named Brash "went to jump on the Cars and missed his hold and fell underneath the Cars and got his leg broken." Stone Diary, 12–13.

They reached Bristol, Virginia, at 9 A.M. on May 15 and remained there until the next morning, when they departed on the Tennessee and Virginia Railroad.

20. John M. Waddill, born in North Carolina about 1840, worked as a clerk before the war. He stood 6'0" with dark eyes and light hair and light complexion. Waddill apparently did not recover fully from his illness at Bristol. He is reported ill at Fredericksburg in November 1861 and had been absent from duty since June 24. He was finally discharged as unfit for service on January 10, 1862. The illness involved his bowels, and his physician reported in December 1861 that he looked like "a walking skeleton." Waddill returned to North Carolina, where he recovered his health and joined the Forty-sixth North Carolina Infantry in March 1862. He served as a quartermaster sergeant until elected

these old towns would be putting it mildly —"red hot" would be about right.[19]

At Bristol John M. Waddill took sick and I was detailed to stay with him at the hotel to which he was carried. He was delirious and kept calling for his mother, who lived in North Carolina. He was a Christian boy and was ready to die, but how natural to want his mother in his distress. But he got better and we resumed our journey to Richmond, where we rejoined our regiment.[20] We camped in the fair ground and were reviewed often by President Davis at dress parade.[21]

I think that to him we must have looked very cheap indeed. We did not know what discipline was and resented being shown. The boys used to steal through the lines and spend most of their time in the city. Bill Barnes drew some pictures of "Company G in Richmond," which caused quite a little trouble at home.[22]

We went from Richmond to Fredericksburg and there camped in the city awhile. We then moved to Brooke's Station, and at this camp had cadets from Richmond to drill us. And I should say they did drill us! Eight hours a day, with a big gun, knapsack and accoutrements weighing us down, the hot sun blazing over us. How we did perspire! We were not used to such strenuous exercise. The town boys, clerks second lieutenant of Company B in September 1864. Waddill survived the war to write a historical sketch of the Forty-sixth North Carolina. Service Records, Roll 52; Walter Clark, ed., *Histories of the Several Regiments and Battalions from North Carolina in the Great War 1861–'65,* 5 vols. (Raleigh: E. M. Uzzell, 1901), III, 63–66.

While Bevens and Waddill remained behind, the remainder of the regiment passed through Wythville, Virginia, where "the Ladies met us with armfills of goodies of all sorts," reported Thomas Stone. They finally reached Lynchburg on May 18 and marched through the town to Camp Davis, located on the fairgrounds a mile from the town. They remained there two weeks, reported Stone, "in a beautiful grove close to one of the finest springs I ever beheld." Bevens and Waddill missed the official mustering into Confederate service on Sunday, May 19, at which time the regiment received Confederate uniforms, canteens, blankets, knapsacks, and other accouterments. On the other hand, they also missed two weeks of drill (three hours every morning, two hours in the afternoon) and camp routine. The weather was lousy, too, with rain much of the first four days in camp. Men slipped into town whenever possible and found themselves to be curiosities. They spent much time "answering questions and telling Arkansas yarns to citizens." As the weather improved, quite a few men spent all their "loose change" at an "Ice Cream saloon" that some enterprising businessman had established inside the camp boundary. Stone Diary, 14–18.

The regiment was informed that it would not be getting the new .58 calibre rifles that had been promised, but would have to make do with older muskets. The men were naturally disappointed, reported Thomas Stone, but they soon "took the news cheerfully. Yes, we would have fought with rocks if nothing else to drive the Yankeys from our homes." Another man expressed a similar reaction. It did not matter, he told his cousin in a letter, how they were armed or where they fought, so long as they fought soon. He had joined the army to fight, and he did not want the war to end before he had done so. As things turned out, the men received their rifles before leaving Lynchburg. Stone Diary, 16–17; Frederick W. Bush to Kate and Emily, 21 May 1861, Frederick W. Bush Letters, Mullins Library, University of Arkansas, Fayetteville.

Meanwhile, drill, routine, and impatience to move to the front produced tensions in camp. A private in Captain Crockett's Company H got in a fist fight with his lieutenant, and a drunken private from a Tennessee regiment shot his lieutenant when the officer reprimanded him for disorderly conduct. Generally, however, the regiment behaved itself as the army slowly assembled. "It will be gratifying, no doubt," a member of the regiment wrote home on May 26, "to hear that there is perfect unanimity, excellent discipline and abundant cheerfulness in the Arkansas Camp. When we first arrived here, the Regiment was somewhat troubled with colds, etc., but there is at present little sickness in camp, and there is an

Capt. A. C. Pickett
First Captain of Company "G",
First Arkansas Infantry

eagerness to meet the worthless intruders from the North, which only grows in intensity as the days wear on. Our men are panting for the fray and, from present indications, they will in a few days get their wishes fulfilled." Stone Diary, 18; *Arkansas Gazette,* 8 June 1861, 2.

21. The regiment arrived at Richmond sometime between May 30 and June 2, although the earlier date seems most likely, and camped about a mile from the city. Col. Jubal A. Early was at least partly responsible for getting the spirited Arkansans out of Lynchburg. On May 27 he wrote to General Robert E. Lee: "There is an Arkansas regiment here, 900 strong, under command Colonel Fagan. . . . It is armed and can be ordered away, which Major Clay, senior officer here of the Confederate Army suggests had better be done, as it is doing no good here." Stone Diary, 19–22; *Arkansas Gazette,* 22 June 1861, p. 2; *The War of the Rebellion: A Compilation of the Official Records of the Union and Confederate Armies,* 70 vols. in 128 books and index (Washington: Government Printing Office, 1880–1901), ser. 1, vol. 51, pt. 2, 115 (cited hereafter as OR, and, unless otherwise indicated, all references are to Series 1).

There is only one recorded instance of Jefferson Davis inspecting the regiment: "On the evening previous to our departure from Richmond, we had the honor of a visit from our beloved President. . . . It was the hour of Dress Parade when he made his appearance on the field. . . . He was on horseback, and appeared before the long line of unpretending but determined soldiers

plainly attired, with no attempt at display—no effort to be imposing." *Arkansas Gazette,* 29 June 1861, 2.

22. It should be noted that Richmond, which had a population of 37,910 (including 11,699 slaves and 2,576 free blacks) in 1860, was not yet the working capital of the Confederacy. The Confederate Congress had voted to move the capital from Montgomery, Alabama, on May 10, but the government did not officially convene in Richmond until June. Long before that, however, the city's fairgrounds had been selected as a training camp, and troops poured into the city by the thousands. Emory M. Thomas, *The Confederate State of Richmond: A Biography of the Capital* (Austin: University of Texas Press, 1971), 32–37. For the impression the city made on one member of the First Arkansas see *Arkansas Gazette,* 22 June 1861, 2. William T. Barnes (1838–1918), son of Nathan Barnes, was born near Elizabeth, Arkansas. He enlisted as a private in Company G. Elsewhere Bevens writes of Barnes, "We were together four years in old Company G and I always found him the most lovable, most genial companion I ever knew." Barnes returned to Jackson County after the war and married seventeen-year-old Emma A. Dooley in 1865. Eventually he moved to Lee County, where he worked forty years for the Western Union Telegraph Company. Bevens, "Makers of Jackson County," 11–12; Ardith Olene Foster, *Marriage and Divorce Records of Jackson County, Arkansas, 1831–1875* (Newport, Ark.: Morgan Books, 1980), 6; *Confederate Veteran* 26 (March 1918), 122.

These winter quarters of the First Texas at Camp Quantico in
1861–62 would have been similar to those of the First Arkansas at
nearby Camp Holmes and on Aquia Creek. *(Courtesy Rosenberg
Library, Galveston, Texas.)*

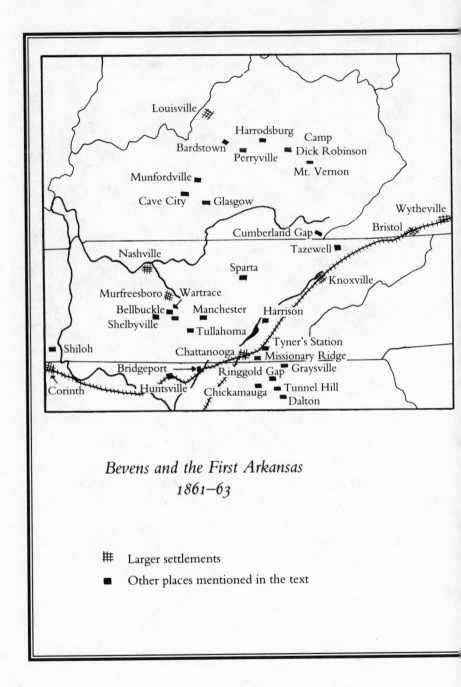

Bevens and the First Arkansas
1861–63

⊞ Larger settlements

■ Other places mentioned in the text

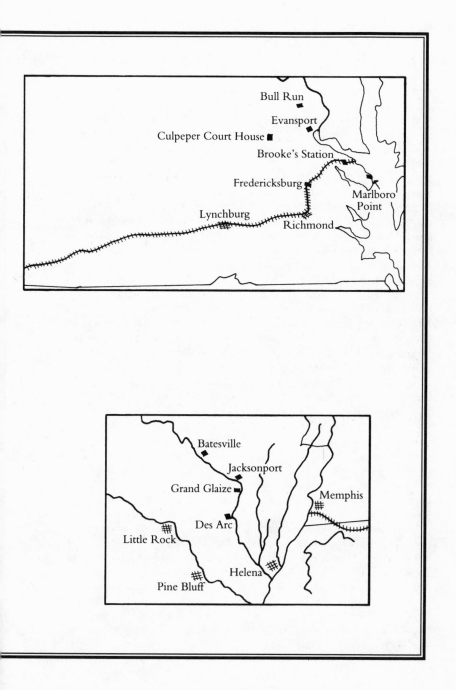

23. The regiment left Richmond about June 3 (Thomas Stone's diary incorrectly says June 6). It passed through Fredericksburg (no source other than Bevens mentions an encampment there, although it is possible that the regiment lingered for a day or so) on the Fredericksburg and Potomac Railroad to Brooke's Station. Here the men established Camp Jackson about five miles west of the mouth of Aquia Creek, an estuary of the Potomac River. Aquia Creek Landing is about fifteen miles northeast of Fredericksburg. The First Arkansas now became part of a brigade (including the Second Tennessee Infantry) commanded by Colonel Daniel Ruggles (1810–97), a native of Massachusetts. Their brigade, in turn, formed part of the Department of Fredericksburg, a force of approximately three thousand under the command of Brig. Gen. Theophilus Hunter Holmes (1804–80). They also heard enemy fire for the first time while at Camp Jackson when some Confederate batteries on Aquia Creek engaged in a duel with the Federal sloop *Pawnee*. Stone Diary, 22–23. For evidence that the regiment was at Camp Jackson by June 4 see OR, vol. 2, 57.

The cadets drilling them were from the Virginia Military Institute and had been summoned to Richmond to serve as drill instructors. Thomas, *Confederate State of Richmond*, 35–36.

A famous incident in the regiment's history occurred at Brooke's Station. That spring, Colonel Fagan had his wife and two children join him in camp. His daughter Irene, age four, quickly found herself adopted as the "Daughter of the Regiment." "The adoption occurred at time of dress parade, the regimental ceremony of the day, the companies in their best attire, the officers in full dress, guns burnished, bayonets gleaming in the sunlight, the sound of music's martial strains caught up in the soft spring air and wafted across Virginia's hills." Rev. R. W. Trimble, regimental chaplain, performed the official "christening" ceremony. Irene later became Mrs. Charles Cockle. About 1905, veterans of the regiment presented Mrs. Cockle with their old regimental flag, the same flag that had been presented to the Jackson Guards in May 1861. She, in turn, presented the flag for safe keeping to the Confederate Museum (now called the Museum of the Confederacy) at Richmond. Laura Govan, "The Daughter of the First Arkansas Regiment," in United Confederate Veterans of Arkansas, ed., *Confederate Women of Arkansas*, 144–45; *Catalogue of the Confederate Museum of the Confederate Memorial Literary Society* (Richmond: Ware & Duke, 1905), 229. The Museum of the Confederacy has confirmed for the editor that the flag is still in its possession. Another source says the ceremony took place in the autumn of 1861, when the regiment was encamped at Evansport, Virginia. See Hammock, *With Honor Untarnished*, 39. On the subject of regimental flags, see chapter 3, note 13.

and young fellows could stand it better than the robust country boys, and that seemed queer to us.[23]

At this camp John M. Waddill took sick with measles. The Regiment lost over fifty men from this disease. Waddill was discharged and went home. After his recovery he joined a North Carolina Regiment, and served with them through the war. He was a gentleman in the truest sense of the word. We hated to lose him.[24] From Brooke's Station we went to Aquia Creek, and from there to Marlboro Point on the Potomac. We camped at a point where this beautiful stream was four miles wide.[25] W. M. Maltens, our company color-bearer waded into the river and unfurled our flag, the handsome silk one given us by the Jacksonport ladies. "Jackson Guards" was very plain upon it, and it was displayed in full sight of the enemy's war vessels. We were lined up on the bank to defend our colors. This shows how green we were in knowledge of warfare and we realized it later.[26]

From Fredericksburg, five companies of our Regiment and five companies of Col. Bate's Second Tennessee Regiment were under Col. Cary. He was a West Pointer, a fine man and officer, but he certainly did drill us eight hours every day.[27] During drill our orderly sergeant, a regular army man, used to prompt us when new moves were given. One

24. Measles was a widespread problem for both armies, especially early in the war. With so many young men thrown together in the close confines of camp life, communicable diseases and sicknesses spread quickly. Concerning the problem at Camp Jackson, General Holmes wrote on June 19, "The Arkansas and Tennessee regiments are suffering very much with measles and diarrhea, and I have caused a large hospital to be prepared in Fredericksburg for them." OR, vol. 51, pt. 2, 141–42. See also Stone Diary, 23.

25. Marlboro Point is on the Potomac River, about five miles downstream from Aquia Point. The move took place about June 28, but Colonel Ruggles had been intending to position the regiment there ("as soon as it is in condition to do so") almost from the day of its arrival at Brooke's Station. Stone Diary, 23; OR, vol. 2, 57, 959.

26. W. H. Maltens should be William H. Mathews. Born about 1829 in Tennessee, Mathews owned a grocery in Jacksonport and, according to the census of 1860, was worth two thousand dollars. He held the rank of private but also served as company ensign (see note 10 above). Mathews was "slightly" wounded in the arm at Murfreesboro and more seriously

wounded at Chickamauga, but he survived the war and returned to Jackson County. He married Mrs. Jerome B. Dennes in 1866. Service Records, Roll 49; Foster, *Marriage and Divorce Records*, 73.

27. William Brimage Bate (1826–1905) was promoted to brigadier general in 1862. His command was the Second Tennessee Infantry Regiment (also called the Second Confederate Infantry), not to be confused with the "Irish Regiment" at Memphis (see note 13 above). After the war, Bate served as the governor of Tennessee and in the U.S. Senate. Wigginton, et al., *Tennessee in the Civil War*, I, 176–78; Warner, *Generals in Gray*, 19–20.

Richard Milton Cary (1824–86) was a Virginia lawyer before the war and does not seem to have been a West Point graduate. He entered service with the First Virginia Infantry and was made colonel of the Thirtieth Virginia in June 1861. The author of a Confederate infantry drill manual, he nonetheless served in the artillery service after June 1862. He emigrated to England after the war. Robert K. Krick, *Lee's Colonels: A Biographical Register of the Field Officers of the Army of Northern Virginia* (Dayton, Ohio: Morningside Bookshop, 1979), 76–77.

A portion of Gibson's brigade (the First Arkansas?) as it attacks the
Hornet's Nest at Shiloh. *(From* Battles and Leaders of the Civil
War, *Vol. I. Copyright by Castle, a division of Book Sales, Inc.)*

28. William D. Shackelford, who served as a private, was a twenty-six-year-old bachelor with a small farm in Jackson County, even though his service record says he was a twenty-year-old tanner. Shackelford was assigned to the Confederate arsenal in Atlanta from November 1863 through August 1864 because of an undisclosed physical disability. He worked in the arsenal as a "laboratorian." Service Records, Roll 51.

morning he was angry at Captain Pickett. When Col. Cary gave the command "Double quick by companies" there was no prompting and Captain Pickett failed to repeat the command. The sergeant had his revenge for we were double-quicking by fours to the line on the right and proceeded by ourselves. Col. Cary shouted "Captain Pickett where are you going with your company?" amid the laughter of the rest of the regiment.

At this camp Bill Shackelford used to go fishing for crabs in the Potomac. He would miss roll-call and have to serve extra duty. The boys begged him to stop this but he said if he could get crabs to eat he did not mind extra duty. One night Bill had some fun at the expense of the officer whose duty it was to pass through the tents and see that all were in bed. We had a big Sibley tent in which twenty-two men slept. As the officer passed through the tent, Bill who was a ventriloquist, squealed like a pig. Of course the officer looked everywhere for the pig. As he passed to the other side of the tent Bill barked like a dog. Then the officer asked for the man that did it. Of course all were asleep and knew nothing about it. He said he would arrest the entire company if it occurred again. Bill did not try it again.[28]

One day Clay Lowe had cooked some corn-bread and left it on the table, feeling that he had done a

29. Henry Clay Lowe enlisted as a private at age nineteen. According to the census of 1860, he had been working as a clerk for Aaron Hirsch, an Independence County merchant worth fifty thousand dollars, with whom he also boarded. Lowe was promoted to sergeant in January 1862, to second lieutenant in April 1862, and to first lieutenant about July 1864. He was one of Bevens's best friends, and he joined Bevens in a business venture shortly after the war. Service Records, Roll 49; Bevens, "Makers of Jackson County," 26.

30. Robert D. Bond, a twenty-two-year-old private who had been born in Tennessee, would be wounded at Shiloh and Atlanta and captured at Nashville (December 16, 1864). He spent nearly five months in Federal prison camps at Louisville and Chicago. He was paroled at Camp Douglas on May 13, 1865, and returned to Jackson County. Bond stood 5'8" and had blue eyes and dark hair. Service Records, Roll 46.

31. Designating "ladies" was a common practice when soldiers sought to amuse themselves with dances. All three men were designated as privates on the company roster, but Billy Barnes and Richard M. Haden were officially detailed as musicians, unlike John Joseph Hamilton. Haden, born about 1840 in Mississippi, was a druggist by profession. He would be "severely" wounded in the thigh at Shiloh. In August 1864 he was assigned to the Medical Department to work as a hospital steward. Hamilton, two years Haden's senior, was a native Arkansan who worked as a gunsmith. According to the census of 1860, Hamilton resided with Eli Stringfellow, an Alabama-born grocer who Bevens says served with Company G, but whose name does not appear on any company muster roll. Hamilton served on detached service as a ward master in the hospital at Dumfries, Virginia, in November and December 1861. He was "slightly" wounded at Shiloh, and in September 1862 he transferred to Morgan's Regiment of Arkansas Volunteers. Service Records, Roll 48.

Two other notable events occurred while the First Arkansas was encamped at Marlboro Point. On July 1, the regiment received its first delivery of letters and packages from home. "We could not be still we were so rejoiced," recorded Thomas Stone. Then, on the evening of July 3, a fierce thunderstorm struck the camp. Rain fell in bucketfuls and tents were blown away, but no one seemed alarmed. Stone reported the men "cracking jokes singing & dancing" during the storm, with the hilarity continuing through the next day. Stone Diary, 24–26.

32. General Holmes had been ordered to Manassas Junction (not Gap) with the First Arkansas, Second Tennessee, and Purcell's Battery by Gen. Pierre G. T. Beauregard, commander of the Army of the Potomac (Confederate), upon the entrance of Brig. Gen. Irvin McDowell's army into northern Virginia. More specifically, the brigade was ordered to Union Mills Ford, on Bull Run Creek, in support of Brig. Gen. Richard Ewell's brigade. Another source says that the brigade marched from Brooke's Station to Union Mills Ford on July 18 and 20. *Confederate Veteran* 3 (January 1895), 22.

good piece of work. After dinner a big man in uniform stepped up and broke open a piece of bread. Clay was about to call him to account in words not very choice, when the big man explained that he was General Holmes, commander of the troops. Clay had to beg his pardon and salute the General, and the General in return complimented Clay on his bread.[29]

At this camp we had jumping matches. Bob Bond was our champion and no one could beat him in the whole command of one thousand troops, and he was never beaten in the army.[30]

We also gave dances, and tied handkerchiefs on the arms of the smallest boys to take the part of ladies in making up square dances. Joe Hamilton, Rich Haden and Billy Barnes were as fine musicians as any and we often had hilarious times along the Potomac.[31]

On July 17, 1861, we were ordered to cook three days' rations, and be ready at daylight to join our regiment and march to Manassas Gap.[32] We marched forty-seven miles and on July 21, were camped in an orchard at the extreme right of our army, with orders to be ready at a moment's notice. We were in line of battle all afternoon and chafed to be in the fight. We could hear the cannonading. It seems that the courier who was bringing our orders to move at once was captured and we did not get the command. "The third time is the charm" and finally the third courier brought news of the battle with orders to

33. One story has it that while waiting in line and listening to the opening stage of the battle of First Manassas (or First Bull Run), the entire brigade burst into a swelling rendition of "Annie Laurie." *Confederate Veteran* 3 (January 1895), 22.

34. Reuben Lindsay Walker (1827–90) commanded Purcell's Battery, which probably had six (not four) guns. He was promoted to brigadier general, as Bevens mentions below, in 1865. Walker, *Generals in Gray,* 322–23; OR, vol. 2, 491.

double-quick eight miles. We made this in one hour and forty minutes. On this hot July day the red dust stirred up by our running made us look like red men. We hardly knew the features of our file leader. While on this run we saw some sizzling looking things streaming through the air. One of the boys said "Captain, what are those things going through the air?" Captain Pickett replied, "You damned fool, you will know soon."[33]

We got there in the nick of time. We were thrown into line of battle and could see in front of us the enemy with glistening bayonets, forward marching, line after line of them. We had a four gun battery, belonging to Holmes' Brigade, commanded by Captain Walker.[34] He was ordered to place his guns on a small hill in our front. He unlimbered and was ready for action. We were ordered to load our guns and lie down behind the battery to protect it if charged. The captain gave the order to fire upon some Yankees who were advancing boldly. As he gave the order he was sitting on his big horse with his feet across the horse's neck. The first shot did not reach the spot; so he got down, sighted the gun himself, and got back on his horse to watch the result. As the shot plowed through the enemy's ranks it looked like cutting wheat, and the Captain said: "Give them hell." The four guns made roads through them and

35. The Black Horse Cavalry was a famous troop of Confederate cavalry that operated at First Manassas under Capt. W. H. Payne as part of the Thirtieth Virginia Cavalry. For its operations during the battle see OR, vol. 2, 532–35.

36. A West Point graduate, Mexican War veteran, and former secretary of war, Jefferson Davis felt compelled personally to inspect the fortunes of his army at Manassas. He galloped from one end of the battle line to the other to congratulate officers and men alike. Bevens may have witnessed a meeting between Davis and Gen. Joseph E. Johnston, who was in overall command of Confederate troops at First Manassas; but he could not have seen Davis and Johnston with General Beauregard because the three men did not confer together until the evening of July 21 in Beauregard's tent. Hudson Strode, *Jefferson Davis: Confederate President* (New York: Harcourt, Brace, 1959), 115–18, 123.

37. Bevens's account of the role of the First Arkansas at First Manassas is fairly accurate. The men could hear the enemy guns nearly all day, but the regiment never fired a shot. General Holmes moved them forward about six miles at 2 P.M., but they arrived on the field too late to participate in the action. "I ordered Walker's rifled guns to fire at the retreating enemy, and Scott's cavalry to join the pursuit," reported Holmes. He reported further that the artillery was "extremely accurate," and that the cavalry pursuit succeeded in "taking many prisoners and capturing much property." OR, vol. 2, 565–66.

Elsewhere, Bevens wrote: "After a double-quick [march] for over eight miles through the most intense heat, we were thrown into line of battle. We could see in front of us the enemy with glistening bayonets, forward-marching, line after line of them." That is when Walker's guns went to work. *Confederate Veteran* 28 (February 1920), 70. For another perspective on the battle, see the letter of Sgt. Wyatt C. Thomas, Company K, in Hammock, *With Honor Untarnished*, 33–35. The best general account of the battle is William C. Davis, *Battle at Bull Run: A History of the First Major Campaign of the Civil War* (Garden City: Doubleday & Company, 1977).

38. The Washington Artillery was the most famous Confederate volunteer artillery unit. First organized in 1838, it was mustered into Confederate service in May 1861. Four batteries fought at First Manassas under Maj. James B. Walton. For Walton's report see OR, vol. 2, 515–18.

with the Infantry on the other flank they could not stand the fire. The Yankees broke in every direction and never did stop. As this was their last stand we moved forward, and the Black Horse Cavalry passed. This was the finest cavalry I ever saw. All the horses were black and the uniforms of the men were handsome to behold.[35] After the Cavalry Johnston, Beauregard and President Davis with all their staff were near us, and the sight was beautiful.[36] We turned the flank of the enemy and the Black Horse Cavalry did the rest. The first battle of Manassas was a great battle and a perfect success.[37]

After the break we were ordered to be down in line of battle and await orders. Part of the Washington Battery was near us. This was an organization of fine boys from New Orleans. After fighting all day they had become separated, part of their battery being in one part of the field, and part in another. After the battle they were hunting their comrades and trying to get the full battery together. Such chatter. Such individual accounts of the battle! They told us of their share in the fight. How they fought the enemy from rear and front and side, and how the Yankees had run off! It was inside history of the battle from privates who were in it.[38] The whole truth of the first battle of Manassas is this: It was fought by undisciplined troops, without previous experience in battle, on a

39. Bevens is mistaken in identifying McDowell's troops as seasoned veterans. They were as green as the Confederates. Lt. Gen. Winfield Scott (1786–1866), a Virginian by birth, was serving as general-in-chief of the Union army when the war began. Age and infirmities led him to resign his post in November 1861.

field they had never trod before. They fought as individuals, and if the officers had not been with them they would have fought just the same.

This was proved, for had they been disciplined troops they would have surrendered when cut off from their command, but not having any better sense they did not know when they were whipped. On this field they fought regular army troops with all the advantage of years and experience. Even our General was doubtful and thought they could not cope with the great army of Scott. But when he saw the Southern boys in action, he saw what, to this day, is the wonder of the world, that we were not to be whipped in six months.[39]

This battle was a hard rap to those who intended to profit by it had it gone the other way. The Grand Army left Washington commanded by the invincible General Scott, having placards on their hats bearing the motto, "On to Richmond." Congressmen, with their wives followed, together with the elite of Washington, all riding in carriages. They also wore badges with the ever-ready slogan, "On to Richmond." They had trunks plastered with the same motto. They carried champagne and were ready for the celebration of a great fete when they should have witnessed the downfall of the Confederacy. Before the battle it was a holiday for them, with their

40. In describing the Washington civilians who gleefully followed the Union army to Manassas for the fun of watching a battle, Bevens tells of one of the more bizarre, yet revealing, episodes of the war. He errs, however, in saying that General Scott personally led the Union army into the field.

41. Confederate troops did not pursue the retreating Federals because they, too, were tired, confused, and disorganized. Jefferson Davis wanted the army to pursue McDowell, but Johnston and Beauregard advised against it. Douglas Southall Freeman, *Lee's Lieutenants: A Study in Command,* 3 vols. (New York: Charles Scribner's Sons, 1942–44), I, 73–80.

42. General Holmes withdrew his command from Manassas on July 22, but if he followed the path described by Bevens, he took an extremely circuitous route. First of all, Dumfries is less than half of the thirty miles Bevens claims they traveled from Manassas. It is also doubtful that the brigade went to Culpeper Court House, which is nearly forty miles from Dumfries with no direct rail link. Evansport (now Quantico),

where the regiment finally halted to establish Camp Holmes, is on a bluff above the Potomac River, about four miles southeast of Dumfries and nearly ten miles north of Aquia Landing.

43. Holmes, now a major general, commanded a division that included units from Arkansas, North Carolina, Virginia, Tennessee, Maryland, and Georgia. By October, there were 3,422 officers and men in the vicinity of Evansport (OR, vol. 5, 933). Brig. Gen. Isaac Ridgeway Trimble (1802–88) directed construction of the battery positions, the first of which were completed on September 29 (OR, vol. 5, 883). In September, the First Arkansas was placed in a brigade with the Second Tennessee and Twelfth North Carolina, under the command of Col. John George Walker (1822–93), a Mexican War veteran from Missouri who would be promoted to brigadier general in 1862. In November, Brig. Gen. Samuel Gibbs French (1818–1910) replaced Trimble as commander of the defenses at Evansport (OR, vol. 5, 851, 952).

wine, and their hope of an easy route of the rebels, and the pleasant anticipation of the capture of soldiers and congressmen of the Confederacy. But after the battle—ah, it was no holiday then! What a blow to their pride was the result. How they tore back to Washington. Their own account of the first battle of Manassas was truly pitiful.[40] We could have easily gone into Washington, but at that time we did not want to go into their territory, all we desired was to defend our own homes, property and states, which were ours according to the constitution.[41]

At daylight we marched to Dumfries, thirty miles back from the station, then to Culpeper court house, and from there to the pine thicket back from Evansport.[42] With us were Captain Walker's battery (Captain Walker afterwards became General of Artillery) and the Thirteenth North Carolina Infantry. With their assistance, working at night with great secrecy, we built batteries to blockade the Potomac, which was only a mile and a half wide at this point. We built three batteries in one mile and mounted large siege guns. The enemy was greatly astonished on the morning we cut the pine thicket and laid our guns open to view.[43]

We next made sail boats and tug boats and schooners. These captured a three masted vessel. When the tugs came towing it to shore we went out

44. On at least one occasion, some members of the regiment (whether from Company G is unknown) set sail on the river in search of Yankee vessels. Their verve drew praise from Lt. Col. John Baker Thompson, Colonel Fagan's second in command: "I believe if our men ever get a chance at the enemy they will do noble work. They are a noble set of men to lead, and I heavily feel my responsibility to them." *Confederate Veteran* 27 (June 1919), 205.

45. Just before Christmas, a private in Company I reported home, "Not a day passes that does not witness an artillery duel between our gunners and the enemy. At times the cannonading becomes quite spirited, and the shells fall thick and fast on both sides. The Yankees, I must accord them the credit to say, shoot well. . . . Not withstanding this, they have thus far done us little damage. Out of the innumerable shots they have aimed at us, not a man on our side has been killed, and but three or four wounded." *Washington* [Arkansas] *Telegraph,* 22 January 1862, 1.

46. General Holmes expressed pleasure with the effectiveness of the blockade and defenses at Evansport. The troops there, he said, had proved "ample for the defense of the heavy batteries on the river against any force the enemy will probably send." As to the condition of the men, he said, "The health of the troops is steadily improving, their discipline excellent, and . . . they are tolerably well instructed." OR, vol. 51, pt. 2, 357–58.

and got it. Later we had a hard time finding a sailor to set the sails. Finally one was discovered in our own company, and as soon as he got on the vessel he ran up the rigging like a genuine sailor. We found the rooms of the captured vessel very fancy. It had a piano on board, and a good deal of nice grub. We unloaded her and then burned her.[44]

We certainly did blockade that river and stop transportation to Washington by way of the Potomac. Then the Yankees built a railroad on the opposite side back from the river and supplied the gap in that manner. We used to bombard the men over there and kill them and their six mule teams. This caused consternation as you may guess.[45]

A small yacht with two on board ran the blockade. Our batteries opened up on them. The balls exploded above and around them, sometimes splashing the water so that we could not see them for the spray. For awhile it seemed as if we had them, but they got through. The yacht was so small that we could not hit it. When they got by, the men waved their hats, as much as to say, "Goodbye", but they never tried to repeat the performance.[46]

One night the enemy ran up a creek by the upper battery, where we had a schooner out and away from the river. In the darkness they passed our guards and burned the schooner. The guards were new recruits

47. Not all contact with the Yanks was hostile. On November 22, one member of the regiment wrote home to say, "Last week some of our men had a conversation with them [the Federals] across the river. They asked if we were not nearly starved. One boy answered that we had enough to live on until we cleaned them out." *Arkansas Gazette,* 14 December 1861, 2.

48. A private in Company H verifies that the First Arkansas started the winter encamped with the Second Tennessee and adds, "We built huts for winter in a valley protected on north by a high hill from which we procured birch and pine poles for houses and fire wood." James L. Nichols and Frank Abbott, eds., "Reminiscences of Confederate Service by Wiley A. Washburn," *Arkansas Historical Quarterly* 35 (Spring 1976), 52–53. But, as will be seen, the First Arkansas was ordered to a new position on Christmas day. One source says that the Second Tennessee was ordered to Stafford Court House in late November. Another source maintains that it was transferred to General French's brigade at Evansport on December 30. In any case, by late December the Tennesseans had been positioned south of Evansport to guard the Potomac between Aquia Creek and the Chopawamsic River. *Arkansas Gazette,* 14 December 1861, 2; OR, vol. 5, 1013.

and very green. They sent to headquarters to ask what they could do. Of course the Yanks had plenty of time to get back to the Potomac. We built huts out of logs, placing them in the side of the hill and roofing them with a foot and a half of earth to keep out the rain. A few of the boys had tents, but I think our log huts were more comfortable, for we covered the floors over with straw. We passed most of the winter here. Our Maryland boys used to cross the river in skiffs at night to visit their homes, and return before daylight.[47]

The Second Tennessee, commanded by Colonel Bate, camped along with us that winter.[48] One day Colonel Bate ordered some work done which did not agree with the dignity of his men. They refused to do it, saying they "were gentle," and asking him to resign. He at once wrote out his resignation and gave it to them. He told them he would as soon be a private as be an officer. That a private must obey, and he was as willing to obey any officer over him as they should be to obey an officer over them. He was a great man, and a fine speaker. At the close of his speech they tore up his resignation and reelected him Colonel.

Colonel Fagan once ordered some boys of our company to set up his tent but they refused. They came back to the company and told us about it, also

49. This incident suggests that the regiment was getting short-tempered as the dullness of camp life and the increasingly cold weather began to wear on the spirits of the men. A soldier in Company E said of the deadening routine, "The same old thing, drill picket, guard, etc. I am tired of it." Frederick W. Bush to Kate and Emily, 8 December 1861, Bush Letters.

50. The snow started to fall in November and remained until February 1862. Nichols and Abbott, eds., "Reminiscences of Confederate Service," 53.

51. George P. Thomas enlisted as a private in Company G, but he would rise through the ranks to become a sergeant major by October 1863. He was wounded at Murfreesboro and killed at Atlanta in July 1864. See Service Records, Roll 52. This is probably the same George Thomas who lived in Independence County and had been born about 1839 in Tennessee. According to the census of 1860, his parents, William and Amanda, had been born in North Carolina, and his father, for whom he clerked, was a merchant worth five thousand dollars.

informed Captain Pickett who went to Colonel Fagan and got them out of it.

So much for raw undisciplined troops.[49]

Christmas was at hand. Our first Christmas in a soldier's camp! How homesick we were as we thought of the people at home and wondered how they were spending Christmas. Here were their boys fifteen hundred miles from them, living in dark huts, wading snow a foot and a half deep. We did not know that the time would come when these dark, rude huts would seem luxurious quarters.[50]

Our mess was composed of George Thomas, Clay Lowe, Bob Bond and myself.[51] George had been left behind at Fredericksburg, where he was ill for some time. He and a private from another company decided to come to camp and spend Christmas with the boys. They left the train and tramped a mile and a half to surprise the mess, arriving in the nick of time. George said they could not bring us turkey, so they brought some whiskey and eggs. They began beating eggs early Christmas morning, and they made a huge pan full of egg-nog. We invited the officers and our friends to take some with us. In the evening the boys went for Col. Fagan and invited him to drink egg-nog. By that time they were pretty full and Clay Lowe told Col. Fagan that he wanted him to understand that he was "Fifth Sergeant of Company

52. John R. Loftin (1838–1919), born near Murfreesboro, Tennessee, had moved with his family to Jackson County in 1849. He was a sergeant in the original company, but in 1862 he was promoted to lieutenant. Loftin, who stood 6'0" and had hazel eyes, black hair, and a fair complexion, resided in Jackson County after the war. He married Betty S. West, the first of two wives, in 1866, when she was seventeen. Service Records, Roll 49; *Confederate Veteran* 28 (February 1920), 70–71; Foster, *Marriage and Divorce Records,* 66.

53. The name of Samuel Shoup does not appear in the 1860 Arkansas census, although there is a J. Shoup living in Jackson County. That Shoup, a saddler worth three thousand dollars, was born in Pennsylvania about 1834. This description fits information contained in Samuel Shoup's service records. Shoup, who would eventually be made captain of Company G, married Nancy Catherine Davis in 1865 in Jackson County. Service Records, Roll 51; *Foster, Marriage and Divorce Records,* 96.

G." He succeeded in impressing the Colonel with his rank. Then everyone began to make things lively.

I did not touch the egg-nog, therefore did not enjoy their hilarity. I left the hut, found Sam Shoup in his hut, and we went out and sat by the fire thinking we were away from the crowd. But the boys did not intend to let us off so easily. When we came back into the hut we could not see very well. The cabin was dark, as the only light came from the doorway, and the snow had blinded us. The boys made a rush for us. I got into a dark corner, and after they were all in we both ran out. They caught Sam, but failed to get me.

Clay Lowe, followed by about twenty-five of the boys, went down to the middle of the company grounds and commenced to make a speech, which he could do so well. Some of the boys, not wishing Clay to have all the glory, put John Loftin on the stump to make an address and he began: "My friends, I am not as eloquent as Clay, but I speak more to the point."[52]

That evening at dress parade, Sam Shoup as corporal had to march out and present arms, reporting two commissioned officers, four non-commissioned officers, and twenty-seven privates drunk.[53] The rest of the regiment was there, and to our consternation, we were ordered to cook three days' rations and be ready to march at daylight. The order read that any

54. The First Arkansas was ordered back to Aquia Creek to replace the Fortieth Virginia, which had been ordered to the Northern Neck of Virginia. OR, vol. 5, 1006, 1012–13, 1018. "Sunday Soldiering" was slang for easy duty, although Bevens almost immediately qualifies this assessment. Depending on their exact position along Aquia Creek, they could not have been closer than nine miles to Fredericksburg, but if positioned near Aquia Creek Station, they would have access to the Fredericksburg & Potomac Railroad, which ran from that point to Fredericksburg.

55. Shortly before Christmas, a private in Company I complained about the meagerness of a soldier's pay and the high cost of living. A Confederate private was paid eleven dollars per month, but prices in the Confederacy had already risen, he estimated, as much as 400 percent since the start of the war. A pair of shoes, "which last only a month," cost five to six dollars. "No one has a proper idea," he elaborated, "without actual experience, of the innumerable little exactions which the soldier is subjected to by the numerous sutlers and hawkers who infest the army. Being unable to procure leave of absence, he is completely at the mercy of these contemptible Shylocks. . . . For a paper of pins or needles, or a skein of thread—which costs from 5 to 7 cents—they charge 25 and 30 cents. For common writing paper, we have to pay 5 cents a sheet; 2 cents apiece for pens and envelopes. And everything else is in proportion." *Washington* [Arkansas] *Telegraph*, 22 January 1862, p. 1.

private who straggled or failed to keep up with the command would be court martialed.

When we stopped late next evening on the march, Clay was nearly dead and could hardly walk, from the effect of the Christmas spree. Colonel Fagan rode along by our company and seeing how Clay was said, "Hello, Fifth Sergeant of Company G, how do you feel?" Clay replied, "Colonel, I am damned dry; how are you?"

December 26, 1861, we reached Aquia Creek and went into winter quarters in log huts and tents. Here we had "Sunday Soldiering." We were close to Fredericksburg, and could order what we wanted to eat.[54] Confederate money was good and we could grab things cheap with it. Fifty cents a gallon for shelled oysters; twenty-five cents a pound for butter; pies and cakes every day. Think of such grub for a soldier![55] But, ah, to stay in the snow, eighteen inches deep, and guard the Potomac river all night! No shelter, but a corn stalk house; no fire, but a driftwood blaze, not very bright either, as it would be a signal for the enemy to cannonade. That was like war and soldier duty.

We had three points to guard on the river, one on the island with battery, and one at the lower end of the line. It required a whole company for all points at night, since the guard had to be relieved every

56. By mid-January, 1862, the
First Arkansas had been brigaded with
the First, Second, and Third North
Carolina State Troops, Thirtieth
Virginia Regiment, Cooke's Battery,
and Walker's Battery. John G. Walker
still commanded them, but he had
been promoted to brigadier general.
OR, vol. 5, 1031.

twenty minutes. Otherwise he would have been frozen by the snow and sleet which swept across the Potomac.[56]

One night a squad from our company under a sergeant was ordered to the island, which was only guarded at night. We had to cross over in a flat boat. The evening before supplies had been sent to the island for the use of the Battery Company and they had failed to haul them. The squad on the lower part of the guard line found them, all unused, in a pile on the landing. The night was bitter cold, the snow was deep, the wind blowing a gale, no wood was in sight. The supplies were bacon. It was good to eat, and in this emergency it was good to burn, so the boys proceeded to burn it. Dawn revealed other things besides bacon. They discovered two jugs of red liquor, which they immediately confiscated. At daylight they were ordered to camp two miles away and proceeded to march—and drink on empty stomachs until the whole squad was drunk. We, on the upper part of the guard line, had to wait in the snow and wind until they came up, for all must report in camp together. We did not know what caused their delay, but we were in no pious frame of mind when we saw them coming, wabbling from side to side, yelling like Comanches. The officers with us were red-headed and said things to that squad that "were bad".

57. Re-enlistment came in February, and most of Company G signed up for the duration of the war in return for a fifty-dollar bonus and a sixty-day furlough. Six men did not re-enlist, most often for reasons of age or health, and another fourteen men had been discharged from the army prior to the expiration of their original enlistment. The regiment was relieved by the Third Arkansas on February 28 and ordered to rendezvous at Memphis on March 15. They proceeded from there to Corinth. Shortly after the regiment's departure from Aquia Creek, the Federal army crossed the Potomac at Evansport, and the remaining Confederate forces fell back toward Fredericksburg.

Before departing Aquia Creek on March 10, the First Arkansas was reviewed by General Holmes, who told the troops—reportedly while shedding a tear—that "he had rather loose [sic] 5 Regiments any time than to loose the 1st Arkansas Regt." The men apparently felt the same way about General Holmes. Colonel Thompson claimed that the regiment "idolized General Holmes," and they had, after all, christened their camp at Evansport "Camp Holmes." Stone Diary, 27–28; *Confederate Veteran* 27 (June 1905), 205.

But the boys from the lower end knew how dry the officers were after being out all night, so they offered the jug of snake bite medicine. The officers found it so good they did not let it go in a hurry. After that the privates could not refuse for fear of making the boys angry. By the time we reached camp almost everybody was overcome. The officers went to sleep, and when they awoke they forgot all about discipline. So nobody suffered but the Battery fellows, and they could never prove who captured their supplies.

Sometimes a company would buy a barrel of oysters, take it to their hut and open it, and find in the center a five gallon jug of red rye. It was so concealed to pass the provost guard on [the] train. But the boys did even worse. Seven of them from other commands, went to Fredericksburg, bought a coffin and filled it with jugs. With sad faces and measured steps they carried it solemnly to the train. But the joke was too good to keep. The boys unscrewed the lid and yelled at the guard. Of course, when the train returned no one could name the offenders.

But our "Sunday Soldiering" did not last long. The regiment was composed of one year troops, who now re-enlisted for three years, or for the war. The re-enlisted men were ordered to rendezvous at Memphis, to reorganize the regiment, but later were ordered to Corinth, Mississippi.[57]

58. Bevens here refers to John R. Fellows, but Fellows never officially held the rank of colonel. An extremely talented and intelligent man, Fellows was appointed acting adjutant of the regiment following the battle of Shiloh, but he did not receive his commission until 1863, when serving on General Beall's staff. Even then, Fellows was only promoted to captain. However, so many unofficial records refer to Fellows as "colonel" that he must have been granted the courtesy of that title by virtue of his position as assistant adjutant to General Beall. Officers' Service Records, Roll 91.

The Virginia people had been good to us, and had tried to make us feel at home. Some of the boys had gone into society at Fredericksburg, and found it hard to part from their new friends. George (my old friend, George Thomas) "had it mighty bad." He said to me, "Bill, I must go to Fredericksburg to see my girl. Will you cook my three days' rations? I'll meet you at the train tomorrow." "But Pard, how will you get off?" "I'll ask Col. Fellows." He went to Colonel Fellows, who was in charge that day and told his tale of woe. The colonel was in deep sympathy with the boy (perhaps he had had the disease himself sometime,) and agreed to help him.[58] George went to Fredericksburg, and the next day I saw him there with his girl. Our train pulled out, I yelled at him, but still he lingered. They gazed and gazed at each other, and it seemed that George did not have the nerve to tear himself away. Finally they parted and by hard running he caught the train and stood waving to her until we were out of sight. The mails were kept hot after that. Poor George was killed at Atlanta. He was the bravest man I ever knew, and if he had lived, would have made that girl a noble husband.

March 17, 1862, at Corinth, Mississippi, the reorganization of the regiment took place. The newly elected officers of Company G were:

59. This election produced rapid promotions for some men. Samuel Shoup and George Sparling had been corporals, and Allie T. Walthall and Forrest W. Dillard had been privates. Three of the men, Sparling, Dillard, and Thomas Davis, are not mentioned again in the text, so the following information is provided here: Forrest W. Dillard (1843–1905) was a brother of Mary Dillard (note 6 above). He did not enlist in the regiment until March 1862, so his promotion was indeed rapid. He was reported absent without leave in January and February 1864, with no further record of military service. A native of Missouri, as was most of his family, he returned to Jackson County after the war and married M. J. Pool, age twenty, in 1867. He became active in the United Confederate Veterans, Camp Tom Hindman, at Newport, Arkansas, and served as camp adjutant. Service Records, Roll 47; Foster, *Marriage and Divorce Records*, 31; *Confederate Veteran* 14 (February 1906), 82.

George Sparling, born about 1837 and a hosteler before the war, enlisted as a private. He was promoted to corporal in November 1861, when John M. Waddill resigned for reasons of health. Service Records, Roll 51.

Thomas B. Davis and his brother, Allen W. Davis, who enlisted in March 1862, were the sons of Col. Matthew and Sarah (Walls) Davis. Both men were wounded at Shiloh. Allen was promoted to sergeant in August 1863. Thomas was also promoted to sergeant, in December 1862, but he was then reduced to private in August 1863 for unexplained reasons. A third brother, Dick, had been too impatient for Jackson County to enter the war and had rushed off to join a Florida regiment before the Jackson Guards could be organized. Tom Davis died of pneumonia at Dalton, Georgia, in 1864; Allen died in 1865 at Bentonville, North Carolina, the regiment's last battle. Their sister, Nancy Catherine Davis, married Samuel Shoup in 1865. Service Records, Roll 47; Bevens, "Makers of Jackson County," *Stream of History* 20 (December 1983), 32.

60. The First Arkansas now became part of an army for the first time, the Army of the Mississippi, commanded by Gen. Albert Sidney Johnston (1803–62) with General Beauregard second in command. They formed part of the Second Army Corps, commanded by Maj. Gen. Braxton Bragg, First Division, commanded by General Ruggles, First Brigade, commanded by Col. Randall L. Gibson. Joining them in the brigade were the Fourth, Thirteenth, and Nineteenth Louisiana regiments, and Vaiden's, or Bain's, Mississippi Battery. OR, vol. 10, pt. 1, 382.

61. The army was supposed to move on April 3, after cooking three days' rations and being issued forty to one hundred rounds of ammunition (accounts of the number vary), but only a portion of the army left on time. Bragg's corps was delayed the better part of a day. Bevens is also correct in stating that the regiment was

Samuel Shoup, Captain.

A. T. Walthall, First Lieutenant.

Clay Lowe, Second Lieutenant.

John R. Loftin, Third Lieutenant.

W. B. Densford, First Sergeant.

Henry Clements, Second Sergeant.

W. H. Reid, Third Sergeant.

George Sparling, Fourth Sergeant.

Thomas Davis, First Corporal.

John W. Baird, Second Corporal.

T. S. Logan, Third Corporal.

Forrest Dillard, Fourth Corporal.[59]

We camped at Corinth, Mississippi, and the army was under General Beauregard until General Albert Sidney Johnston arrived.[60] April 4th we marched to Shiloh, arriving there April 5th. The constant rains had made the roads so bad that we had to pull the cannon by hand as the horses mired in the mud.[61] But by this time we were used to hardships, and nothing discouraged that superb commander, General Albert Sidney Johnston. Every soldier loved him and was ready to follow him to the death. At the battle of Shiloh we were placed in the Gibson Brigade, Bragg's Division. On the night before the battle the Medical Department ordered six men from each company to report to headquarters for instructions. I was one of the six to report from our company. The Surgeon

not finally in position until the late afternoon of April 5. Torrential rains and rough terrain slowed the pace of advance. Wiley Sword, *Shiloh: Bloody Sunday* (New York: William Morrow & Company, 1974), 98–101; James Lee McDonough, *Shiloh—in Hell before Night* (Knoxville: University of Tennessee Press, 1977), 80–81; Grady McWhiney, *Braxton Bragg and Confederate Defeat* (New York: Columbia University Press, 1969), 225.

L. C. Gause
First Lieutenant Company "G",
First Arkansas Infantry

62. Johnston had also penned a brief, stirring address to be read to each regiment as the army advanced on April 3–5. Additionally, just before advancing on April 6, Johnston confided to Bevens's brigade commander, Colonel Gibson, "I hope you may get through safely to-day, but we must win a victory." McDonough, *Shiloh,* 78–79; William Preston Johnston, "Albert Sidney Johnston at Shiloh," in Robert Underwood Johnson and Clarence Clough Buel, eds., *Battles and Leaders of the Civil War,* 4 vols. (New York: Century Company, 1887), I, 557.

63. William H. Scales was originally a lieutenant in the Camden Knights, Ouachita County, which became Company C in the First Arkansas.

General ordered us to leave our guns in camp and follow behind the company and six paces, as an infirmary corps to take care of the wounded. We reported our instructions to Captain Shoup, telling him we would not leave our guns, as we intended to fight. After hard pleading Captain Shoup consented. We took our guns and also looked after the wounded.

At four o'clock in the morning [April 6] we began the march on the enemy. Each man had forty cartridges, all moving accoutrements and three days' rations. General Johnston was cheered as he rode by our command and I remember his words as well as if they had been today, "Shoot low boys; it takes two to carry one off the field."[62]

Before we started Captain Scales of the Camden Company, begged his negro servant to stay in camp at Corinth, but the old negro would not leave his master. When we were in line of battle the captain again begged the negro to return to camp, but he refused to go. Just after the last appeal the fight began. A cannon ball whizzed through the air and exploded, tearing limbs from trees, wounding the soldiers. One man fell dead in front of the old negro. Then there was a yell, and old Sam shouted, "Golly, Marster, I can't stand this," and set out in a run for Corinth.[63]

64. Thadious D. Kinman was born in Batesville in 1844. In 1860 he resided in Jackson County in the home of R. Kinman, a steamboat captain who had been born in Kentucky. A steamboat pilot by the name of J. Kinman, also from Kentucky, lived next door. Thadious Kinman enlisted in the Seventh Arkansas when just sixteen and worked in the paymaster and supply departments. He returned to Jacksonport after the war and worked in the steamboat business and as a bookkeeper. He married Mary E. Dillard in 1867. *Biographical and Historical Memoirs of Northeast Arkansas,* 878–79.

65. This is probably James W. Stimson (also spelled Stimpson), born in North Carolina about 1842 (although other implied dates are 1822 and 1838). According to the census of 1860, his father, M. Stimson, was a prosperous, Virginia-born farmer in Jackson County, worth nearly twenty-eight-thousand dollars. However, if it is Stimson to whom Bevens refers, he is mistaken about his death at Shiloh. Stimson died at Jonesboro in 1864, and offers an instance of the awkward way in which relatives often heard of the death of their soldiers. "I wish you would send word to James Stimpsons sisters," wrote a member of Company G to his father, "that he is killed or at least was mortialy wounded and fell into the enemys hands and it is thought he is dead." Service Records, Roll 51; John A. McDonald to Alvin McDonald, 28 September 1864, in "Civil War Letter of John McDonald," *Stream of History* 2 (October 1964), 12.

We moved forward with shot and shell, sweeping everything before us. We drove the officers from their hot coffee and out of their tents, capturing their camp and tents. Captain Shoup and John Loftin and Clay Lowe each got a sword. In the quartermaster's tent we found thousands of dollars in crisp, new bills, for they had been paying off the Yankee soldiers.

Thad Kinman of the 7th Arkansas, who was under Ellenburg, quartermaster department, had loaded a chest into a wagon when he was ordered to "throw that stuff away." He told us afterwards, "That was one time that I was sick," but Ellenburg would not let him keep it.[64]

Our command moved steadily forward for a mile or more. The Yankees had time to halt the fleeing ones, form a line of infantry and make a stand in an old road in a thicket. We were to the left of the thicket, fighting all the time in this part of the field. I saw Jim Stimson fall, and being on the Infirmary Corps, I went to him. I cut his knapsack loose and placed it under his head, tied my handkerchief about his neck, and then saw that he was dead.[65] I took up my gun again, when in front I saw a line of Yankees two thousand strong, marching on the flank. I could see the buttons on their coats. I thought I would get revenge for my dead comrade, so I leveled beside a tree, took good aim at a Yankee, and fired. About

66. Bragg's corps followed the corps of Maj. Gen. William Joseph Hardee in order of battle. Colonel Gibson's brigade was positioned precisely in the middle of the Second Corps, and the First Arkansas went into action in the right center of the brigade. Colonel Fagan, in his after action report, stressed the difficulty of the terrain—it was heavily wooded and studded with thickets—and the fatigue of his men after their three-day march. The regiment first encountered enemy fire while filing through an open field a short distance from the Union camp, probably against the Twelfth and Fourteenth Iowa Infantry. After a skirmish, the enemy fell back. About an hour later, as the regiment's advance continued, a second fire fight took place. The major encounter, stressed by Bevens, found the Federals falling back into the famous Sunken Road, an old wagon trace that served as the principal Union defense in the fighting on April 6. Here, facing the very heart of the Union line, the regiment marched across a wheat field, into "a dense thicket of undergrowth" and "down to a ravine and a hill beyond." Three times the regiment threw itself at the "Hornet's Nest," or, as the Arkansans called it, the "Butcher's Pen," where it faced a "murderous fire until endurance ceased to be a virtue." So confused and murderous was the fighting that at one point the First Arkansas believed it was being fired upon by the Fourth Louisiana, part of its own brigade. Capt. H. M. Favrot, of the Delta Rifles, reported receiving a message from Colonel Fagan which pleaded, "For God's sake to cease firing; that we were killing his men and he was killing ours." Some portions of the brigade attempted a fourth advance, but they could not crack the Yankee line. The "cannonading" referred to by Bevens must, indeed, have "fairly shook the ground." The Confederates unleased the largest concentration of artillery firepower— sixty-two guns—used in battle in North America to that time. OR, vol. 10, pt. 1, 487–89; Sword, *Shiloh*, 247–56.

that time the Yankees fronted and fired. Hail was nothing to that rain of lead. I looked around and found only four of our company. One was dead, two were wounded and I was as good as dead I thought, for I had no idea I could ever get away. To be shot in the back was no soldier's way, so I stepped backward at a lively pace until I got over the ridge and out of range, assisting the wounded boys at the same time. I had not heard the command to oblique to the right and close up a gap, and that was how we four happened to be alone in the wood. But I did some running then, found my regiment at the right of the thicket and fell into rank. When I got there the company was in a little confusion through not understanding a command, whether they were to move forward or oblique to the right. Captain Shoup thought his men were wavering, so he stepped in front of the company, unsheathed his new sword and told the boys to follow him. He had scarcely finished with the words when a bullet struck his sword and went through wood and steel. The boys were redheaded. They told him he did not have to lead them. They were ready to go anywhere. So we went forward into the hottest of the battle where the roar of musketry was incessant, and the cannonading fairly shook the ground.[66] Men fell around us as leaves from the trees. Our regiment lost two hundred and

67. The regiment actually lost 364 men (killed, wounded, and missing), about a third of its total strength. Among the dead was Colonel Thompson, his body pierced by seven balls. Company G had 4 men killed, 18 wounded, and 1 missing. The brigade lost 97 dead, 488 wounded, and 97 missing. The loss of General Johnston, as suggested by Bevens, was a brutal blow to the South. The episode of his death has been retold many times. He had suffered a serious but not necessarily fatal leg wound. However, he bled to death before a surgeon could attend him, either because his aides did not know how to halt the flow of blood or because they they were unaware of the seriousness of the wound. Charles P. Roland, *Albert Sidney Johnston: Soldier of Three Republics* (Austin: University of Texas Press, 1964), 338.

The First Arkansas bedded down on the night of April 6 in the original Yankee camp, "worn with fatigue, decimated in numbers, but elated that such a hard-fought day had such a glorious close." OR, vol. 10, pt. 1, 488.

68. Federal reinforcements (about 23,000) arrived during the night of April 6–7 under Brig. Gen. Don Carlos Buell and Brig. Gen. Lewis Wallace. Two gunboats accompanied them. The First Arkansas fell into line of battle at about 7 A.M. on April 7. Positioned again on the brigade's far right, the regiment advanced against Thurber's Missouri Battery. They seized one of the Federal guns, but were forced to abandon it "under a brisk fire from the enemy, who were concealed in numbers in the woods beyond." Bevens, Loftin, and Waddill were probably wounded in this exchange (see below). The entire brigade then retired into a ravine, apparently by order of General Beauregard, who feared that Colonel Gibson's men were in danger of being outflanked. But an hour later, the brigade was thrown against the Union line further to the right, near Water Oaks Pond. They failed to break through. "They rallied around their colors and pressed on time and again," boasted a proud Colonel Fagan of his regiment, "until they were forced to retire by the overwhelming pressure against them." Sword, *Shiloh*, 406–09; OR, ser. 1, vol. 10, pt. 1, 488–89.

69. John A. Cathey (1841–1919), born at Raleigh, Tennessee, moved to Jackson County in 1859. He was "slightly" wounded in the arm at Shiloh. After fighting through the entire war as a private, he returned to Jackson County where he became a successful businessman at Catheytown. He married eighteen-year-old Sarah Roberts in 1866. Service Records, Roll 46; *Confederate Veteran* 28 (February 1920), 70; Foster, *Marriage and Divorce Records*, 20.

James Bruce Waddill was apparently an orphan. Born in Arkansas about 1840, he lived with the family of a prosperous Kentucky-born farmer named J. Robinson (worth eighty

seventy, killed, wounded and captured. The battle raged all day and when night came the enemy had been pushed back to the verge of the Tennessee river. But our victory had been won at great price, in the loss of our beloved General, Albert Sidney Johnston, who was killed early in the action.[67]

General Beauregard, next in command, succeeded Johnston, and the battle opened again at daylight the next morning [April 7]. During the night the enemy had been strongly re-inforced, and our men were steadily pressed back.[68]

John Cathey, John R. Loftin, Waddill and I were among the wounded. We were sent to the field hospital several miles back in the wood. When the Surgeon General went to work on me he gave me a glass of whiskey, saying it would help me bear the pain. I told him I would not drink it. He then handed me a dose of morphine. I refused that. He looked me squarely in the face, saying, "Are you a damned fool?"[69]

Our men, fighting stubbornly all the while, were pushed back by superior force through and beyond the Yankee camps we had captured so easily the day before, and at last retreated to Corinth, amidst a terrible storm of rain and sleet. We had lost about ten thousand men. That was the beginning of our real soldiering and the greatest battle we had been in.

thousand dollars). Bevens elsewhere claims that Waddill was the son of J. J. Waddill, an early pioneer and long-time sheriff of Jackson County. Waddill was "seriously" wounded in the right leg at Shiloh on April 7. Captured by the Federals, he had his leg amputated at the thigh by a Yankee doctor in Covington, Kentucky, on May 5. He was exchanged a few months later and promptly furloughed. Waddill spent most of the rest of the war in Jackson County, where he married Ladona E. McCoy in 1864. Service Records, Roll 52; Bevens, "Makers of Jackson County," 8–9; "Return of Maimed Soldiers of Jackson County, Arkansas, 1867," *Stream of History* 13 (April 1975), 25; Foster, *Marriage and Divorce Records,* 109.

Clay Lowe
Second Lieutenant Company "G",
First Arkansas Infantry

70. Actual total losses were 23,741: 13,047 for the Federals, 10,694 for the Confederates. Shiloh was one of the toughest fights experienced by Company G and the First Arkansas. Company G lost two men dead and two captured, and twenty-one men were wounded. Before retiring to Corinth, Mississippi, the regiment encamped at Monterey, Tennessee, the site of their encampment the day prior to the battle. "Night closed upon us," reported Colonel Fagan, "tired and foot-sore, but not dispirited." OR, vol. 10, pt. 1, 489.

71. Soon after arriving at Corinth, Bragg was forced to reorganize his battered corps. The First Arkansas found itself in the Fourth Brigade, commanded by Col. J. C. Moore, and part of Benjamin Franklin Cheatham's division. The brigade's other regiments were the Second Texas and Fifty-first Tennessee. OR, vol. 10, pt. 2, 461.

72. The Farmington engagement occurred on May 9 about four miles east of Corinth. Colonel Fagan led elements of the First Arkansas and Second Texas and a section of William H. Ketchum's Alabama Battery. Capt. William A. Crawford directed the First Arkansas in the fight. He saw his men capture a Federal lieutenant, sergeant, and three privates. OR, vol. 10, pt. 1, 829–30.

About thirty thousand men were killed, wounded and captured in those two days, the loss on each side being fifteen thousand.[70]

At Corinth we awaited re-inforcements and prepared to renew the struggle.[71] The Yankee forces advanced to Farmington, and we had a little more fighting. They captured one of our outposts, then we drove them back to their lines. Colonel Fellows was always on the front line. At this battle he plunged after some cavalry, following them he struck low, boggy ground. He got stuck in the mud and lost his hat, but succeeded in capturing the enemy.[72]

We kept heavy guards at night. One night eighteen of our company were put on out-post, but our cavalry was still further out. George Thomas and I were stationed inside a fence row. We were told not to fire, and we were to be relieved before daybreak. We were not relieved however, and when day came we found ourselves only a short distance from the Yankee breastworks. We could have kept concealed by the grass and bushes, but George, who knew not the meaning of fear, stood in his corner of the fence-row. As he watched the Yankees walking their beats on the breastworks he thought it a good opportunity, and before I knew it, he had shot his man. Oh, then three cannon and two thousand infantry turned loose on us! The fence was knocked to smithereens. The

73. Thomas Stone told of another picket incident on May 3. A portion of Company G was on picket with an Arkansas cavalry battalion and a Tennessee infantry regiment. When they found themselves about to be outflanked by a Federal advance, the First Arkansas wanted to stand and fight, but the other detachments "took to the wood and told us to follow them." The men of Company G hesitated, but seeing no other solution, they followed the "cowardly Devils." Stone Diary, 36. The Tennessee unit may have been the Thirty-ninth Tennessee Infantry Regiment. See Wigginton, et al., *Tennessee in the Civil War,* I, 255–58.

rails, filled with bullets, crashed over us. Limbs falling from trees, covered us, and we were buried beneath the debris like ground hogs. We could not get out until darkness fell again. Then we found some of our cavalry, and tried to get back to our regiment, but the Yanks were between us and our command. The cavalry said we could fight our way through their lines, and we did. The cavalry soon left us behind. Yankees were shooting all around us and yelling for us to surrender, but we ran into a ravine, where we were hidden by the thick undergrowth, and so we got away.[73]

1. Beauregard disguised his withdrawal to avoid a close Federal pursuit
by leaving a skeletal force in the city
and by sending "deserters" into
Federal lines to report the anticipated
arrival of reinforcements. "Who
struck Billy Patterson" is a popular
phrase of the period used to express
bafflement or suggest a mystery. The
evacuation on May 29 also provided
an opportunity for six men to desert
Company G. The company's first
deserter had fled during the withdrawal from Shiloh. A total of
twenty-one men deserted Company
G during the war, nine in 1862, four
in 1863, and eight in 1864.

Chapter Two

ON May 29, 1862, General Beauregard evacuated Corinth. We retreated on a dark night through a densely wooded bottom road. About two o'clock we halted. As soon as we stopped we dropped in the road anywhere, anyhow, and were fast asleep. Some devilish boy got two trace chains and came running over the sleeping men, rattling the chains, yelling "Whoa! Whoa!" at the top of his voice. Of course all the commotion—we had it then. Soldiers grasped the guns at their sides, officers called, "Fall in, fall in men." When the joke was discovered it would have been death to that man, but no one ever knew "who struck Billy Patterson."[1]

We marched forty miles and camped at Twenty Mile Creek on the Mobile and Ohio railroad. On

2. Tupelo is about fifty miles south of Corinth on the Mobile and Ohio Railroad, but the army arrived there on June 9, not June 5. The army underwent extensive reorganization at Tupelo, beginning with the replacement of Beauregard by Gen. Braxton Bragg (1817–76). Colonel Fagan was transferred to cavalry duty in Arkansas. He was replaced as regimental commander by Col. John W. Colquitt. Colquitt, the beneficiary of an antebellum education at a Georgia military academy, had begun the war as a lieutenant in the Monticello Guards, Drew County, Arkansas, that became Company I of the First Arkansas. In February 1862, he had been promoted to major and placed on the regimental staff. Colquitt had been so severely wounded at Shiloh that he had been sent home to Monticello to recuperate. The regiment was still part of the Second Corps, but Maj. Gen. Samuel Jones had replaced Bragg as corps commander. General Walker still led their brigade (the Third), but they now served with the Twenty-first Louisiana, Thirteenth Louisiana, Thirty-eighth Tennessee, Crescent (Louisiana) Infantry, Lumsden's Alabama Battery, Barret's Missouri Battery, and an independent Tennessee regiment. By naming James Patton Anderson as his division commander, Bevens is anticipating a further reorganization that occurred at Chattanooga. At Tupelo, however, the Second Corps was not yet formally divided into divisions, and

Anderson was the commander of the First Brigade. John C. Hammock, *With Honor Untarnished: The Story of the First Arkansas Infantry Regiment, Confederate States Army* (Little Rock: Pioneer Press, 1961), 50, 60, 70; *The War of the Rebellion: A Compilation of the Official Records of the Union and Confederate Armies,* 70 vols. in 128 books and index (Washington: Government Printing Office, 1880–1901), ser. 1, vol. 10, pt. 1, 788 (cited hereafter as OR, and, unless otherwise indicated, all references are to Series 1).

Bragg began sending troops out of Tupelo on July 22, bound for Chattanooga and the beginning of his Kentucky campaign. A total of thirty thousand troops followed the circuitous route mentioned by Bevens through Mobile, Montgomery, Atlanta, and Dalton, Georgia. See Grady McWhiney, *Braxton Bragg and Confederate Defeat* (New York: Columbia University Press, 1969), 268–70.

3. Peter Snyder, of Pocahontas, Arkansas, commanded the Sixth Arkansas Infantry and later, when casualties had begun to take their toll, the Sixth and Seventh Arkansas (Consolidated).

4. The Battle House was one of the finest hotels in the South. Mobile, which started the war with a population of about 29,000 (including about 8,400 blacks), had been largely taken over by the military by the summer of 1862. One resident wrote in late May, "The city is quite deserted. Nearly all

June 5th we reached Tupelo. We were put in Anderson's Division of General Walker's Brigade and camped at Tupelo until August 4th, when we were ordered to Montgomery, Ala.[2]

We went on the train to Mobile. Here I went up into the city with Colonel Snyder and two of his friends, I being the only private among them.[3] It seemed ages since we had enjoyed a square meal. We went into a fine restaurant near the Hotel Battle House, four half-starved Confederate soldiers. Just at the smell of oyster stew I collapsed. But we ordered everything—oysters raw, fried, stewed, fresh red snapper; just everything. We ate. I hope we ate! I think that proprietor was astounded, but it was only our pocketbooks that suffered.[4] At last when we could eat no more, we had fine cigars, and as Dr. Scott said later, "This was good enough for a dog."[5]

We went from Mobile to the railroad station on the bay, where the water flows under the platform. The train was two hours late, so the boys shed their clothes, and in ten minutes there were a thousand men in the bay. They swam about splashing, kicking, diving, having fun until some of the boys went in where the palm flags were growing and espied a large alligator with his mouth wide open. In less time than it takes to tell it there was not a soldier in the bay. Strange! Men, who had stood firm in battle, had the families that could have left for the interior. The town is quite a military camp at present and still it is very quiet and pleasant and everyone feels perfectly safe." Cora Weekes to Nicholas Weekes, 30 May 1862, in Sidney Adair Smith and C. Carter Smith, Jr., eds. *Mobile: 1861–1865. Notes and a Bibliography* (Chicago: Wyvern Press, 1964), 10.

5. Thomas J. Scott (1838–1906) was born in Alabama and studied medicine in Mississippi and Louisiana. He practiced medicine before the war at Arkadelphia, Arkansas. He enlisted in Company A, First Arkansas, but when called from the battlefield at First Manassas to attend the wounded he remained in service as a surgeon. After the war, he practiced medicine in Arkansas and Texas. *Confederate Veteran* 15 (November 1907), 514.

Confederate rifle pits such as these on Kenesaw Mountain would have protected the First Arkansas as it repulsed Sherman's attack in late June 1864. *(Courtesy Massachusetts Commandery Military Order of the Loyal Legion and the U.S. Army Military History Institute.)*

6. Montgomery, Alabama, was a pleasant town of nine thousand people (half white, half black) in 1860. It had served as the Confederate capital from February to May 1861. Mary Chesnut, whose husband served in the Confederate Congress at Montgomery, found the town a better place to visit than to live in: "Flies and mosquitoes and a want of neatness and a want of good things to eat did drive us away." C. Vann Woodward, ed., *Mary Chesnut's Civil War* (New Haven: Yale University Press, 1981), 94.

7. William E. Arnold (1840–1923) hailed from Prescott, Arkansas. He attended Atlanta Medical College just prior to the war. Having first enlisted as a private in Virginia, he transferred to the Army of Mississippi in 1862 and fought at Shiloh. Shortly thereafter, having been promoted to captain and assistant surgeon, he was assigned to the First Arkansas. He practiced medicine in Prescott after the war. Mary Davis Woodward, "Dr. W. E. Arnold—A Personality Sketch," *Arkansas Historical Quarterly* 8 (Winter 1949), 331–35.

8. The watermelons were forbidden because authorities feared they would produce severe cases of diarrhea, already a substantial problem in the army. But more than just the watermelon trade was being regulated in Atlanta. Atlanta, with a population of ten thousand people (mostly white), became a permanent military installation in May 1862. A series of orders, regulating the civilian and military populations alike, swiftly followed. By late May, one Atlanta resident complained in his diary, "Our city is in a measure under Martial law now, and we have all had to obtain passes to prevent our being taken up at night and put in limbo." When Bragg's army arrived in August, the city came officially under martial law. All "intoxicating liquors" were forbidden to soldiers, and any civilian caught selling them to the troops without "the order of an army surgeon" would be taken into custody. Franklin M. Garrett, *Atlanta and Environs: A Chronicle of Its People and Events,* 3 vols. (1954; Athens: University of Georgia Press, 1969–87), I, 525–27; *Atlanta Southern Confederacy,* 8 August 1862, 1.

faced cannon, had endured shot and shell, now fled from one alligator!

We went by rail to Montgomery, where we arrived August 7th. We went into camp near the river and had a chance to swim without fear of alligators.

Montgomery, as the first capital of the Confederacy, was a noted place and many celebrated people lived there.[6] Dr. Arnold and I had bought ourselves "boiled" white shirts, thinking we might be invited into society, but we seemed to have been forgotten by the "haut ton." But it was a beautiful city and we inspected it thoroughly. We were too many for the police, so they "gave us rope to hang ourselves."[7]

We went on next day to Atlanta. When we got there we hoped to eat a big Georgia watermelon, but to our consternation, found the provost guard destroying every watermelon in the city. They were fresh, red and juicy and made our mouths water, but discipline had improved and we touched not, handled not the unclean watermelons. The doctor said they would make us sick. Citizens and negroes might eat them. For soldiers they were sure poison.[8]

We passed up the Sequatchee Valley with its fine springs, stone milk houses, and rich bottom land. We camped on Cumberland Mountain and we camped on Caney Fork. We marched thirty-five miles to

9. Bond evidently did not find his Tennessee belle as sweet as Fannie Board, back in Jacksonport. He and Fannie corresponded during the war, and were wed at Jacksonport in October 1865. Lady Elizabeth Watson, *Fight and Survive!* (Conway, Ark.: River Road Press, 1974), 133; Ardith Olene Foster, *Marriage and Divorce Records of Jackson County, Arkansas, 1831–1875* (Newport, Ark.: Morgan Books, 1980), 11. Wartime romances do not seem to have been a rare event in Company G. Bevens mentions one involving George Thomas earlier in the text (p. 61) and others will follow. See also Thomas R. Stone Diary, pp. 19–20, 30–31, Arkansas History Commission, Little Rock. John A. McDonald, a private in Company G, was courting a girl in Georgia in 1864. He spoke of marrying her but never did. Interestingly, at the time of this flirtation, McDonald sent a warning to his sister to beware of wartime romances: "Tell sister not to let a man fool her to wait until this war is over, tell her that there is no confidence to be placed in a soldier for I no that by experience though I never fooled a lady yet nor never intend to." John A. McDonald to Alvin McDonald, 28 September 1864, in "Civil War Letter of John A. McDonald," *Stream of History* 2 (October 1964), 11.

10. After traveling to Chattanooga by rail from Tupelo, Bragg's army had to march the rest of the way through Tennessee and Kentucky. His first infantry units arrived at Chattanooga on July 29, but it was another month before his entire force had rendezvoused. The Army of the Mississippi departed from Chattanooga on August 28, but to date precisely the movements of individual units thereafter is difficult. However, by September 14 Bragg's "entire army, 'footsore and tired,' rested at Glasgow." The total distance traveled from Chattanooga to Glasgow, Kentucky, was about 150 miles. Thomas L. Connelly, *Army of the Heartland: The Army of Tennessee, 1861–1862* (Baton Rouge: Louisiana State University Press, 1967), 221–28; McWhiney, *Braxton Bragg*, 271, 277, 281–84. The route of Bragg's army is clearly marked in Calvin D. Cowles, comp., *Atlas to Accompany the Official Records of the Union and Confederate Armies* (Washington: Government Printing Office, 1891–95), Plate XXIV.

The army was reorganized at Chattanooga before marching northward to join forces with Maj. Gen. Edmund Kirby Smith. The First Arkansas was assigned to Col. Samuel Powell's Third Brigade, Brig. Gen. James Patton Anderson's Second Division, Maj. Gen. William Joseph Hardee's Second Corps. Also serving under Powell in the Third Brigade were the Forty-fifth Alabama, Twenty-fourth Mississippi, Twenty-ninth Tennessee, and Capt. O. W. Barrett's Missouri Battery.

Sparta, Tennessee, and camped, and there we were ordered to wash our clothes and to cook three days' rations. All this marching was on the famous Bragg Kentucky Campaign and the old general trained us to walk until horses could not beat us. We marched eleven, twelve, thirteen————fifty miles. We waded the Cumberland river, and it was very swift and deep. My messmate, Bob Bond, found a sweetheart here, but he could not tarry and they parted in tears.[9] We camped at Red Sulphur Springs, marched thirty-eight miles and camped on the Tennessee and Kentucky line. We passed through Glasgow, marching all night.[10] These forced marches were hard on us, seasoned infantry as we were. Dr. Arnold, my file leader said:

"Bill, I can't go any further, don't you see I go to sleep walking? I can't stand it any longer."

"You're no good," I replied, "you can stand it as well as I can, besides if you leave the road you will be captured and will have to eat rats."

"Goodbye, old friend, I am gone," was his answer. He ran into the wood twenty or thirty feet from the road, dropped down and was asleep by the time he hit the ground.

He said when he awoke he heard sabres clashing and cavalry passing. He thought he "was a goner", but he soon heard the familiar voice of General

11. William Joseph Hardee (1815–73), of Georgia, was a West Point graduate and a veteran of the Mexican War. He had a reputation for being a soldier's general, much admired by his men, as Bevens's account will soon demonstrate.

12. A premature attack on Munfordville, Kentucky, by Bragg's lead brigade failed on September 14, but as the rest of the army arrived, the Federal garrison of 4,133 men was completely surrounded. When asked to surrender, the Federal commander, Col. John T. Wilder, an Indiana industrialist with no military experience, asked for proof of the size of Bragg's army. Bragg responded that he would prove the size of his army by attacking. Wilder decided to capitulate on September 17.

Hardee. He was calling to get up and go on. He said even a soldier's endurance had a limit, and that limit was now reached. We would not go much further without a rest. Then he ordered his body guard to charge the sleeping men. Dr. Arnold had to run for his command or be court martialed. Panting for breath, he joined us after we had gone into camp, and exclaimed, "Bill, I wish I had come on, for I am nearly dead, and old General Hardee is after me hot and heavy."[11]

On September 17th we left Cave City at daybreak, and marched fifteen miles to Munfordville, which we surrounded, placing a battery on every hill and knoll that commanded the town. We had eighty cannon ready to open fire, and then demanded the surrender of the garrison, and on September 18th six thousand men marched out, laying down six thousand guns.[12] While Will Reid of our company was loading guns into a wagon, one went off accidentally and shot off his arm. General Hardee was riding over the battle-field, and seeing Reid with his arm dangling at his side asked his staff surgeon, Dave Yandell, "Who is that man's surgeon?" Yandell pointed out Dr. Young. Dr. Young had gone out in our company a graduate surgeon. He was young and up to that time he had made no operation of note. He begged the staff-surgeon to help him, but Yandell refused, saying he

13. William H. C. Reid, a private, was born in Tennessee about 1840. His family, which included an older sister and two younger brothers, had moved to Independence County, Arkansas, in 1850. A clerk by occupation, Reid stood 5'10" and had blue eyes, light hair, and a light complexion. The accident occurred on September 22, and his arm was amputated that same day by Dr. Young. Reid was left at Munfordville when the army withdrew. He was subsequently captured by the Federals and sent to Cairo, Illinois. He was released in December 1862 and rejoined the regiment. Compiled Service Records of Confederate Soldiers Who Served in Organizations from the State of Arkansas, National Archives Microcopy 317, Roll 51 (hereafter cited as Service Records); "Return of Maimed Soldiers of Jackson County, Arkansas, 1867," *Stream of History* 13 (April 1975), 25.

David W. Yandell was made medical director of General Hardee's corps in December 1862. Rawlings Young, born about 1835, enlisted in Company G as a private but was appointed assistant surgeon in July 1861. He passed his medical board examination and was appointed surgeon in July 1862 at Tupelo; he was officially posted to the First Arkansas as a surgeon in December 1862, although he had been serving as regimental surgeon since September. Service Records, Roll 52; James Logan Morgan, ed., *Independence County, Arkansas, Seventh Census Free Population Schedules 1850* (Newport, Ark.: Northeast Arkansas Genealogical Association, 1971), 52; Joseph Jones, "Roster of the Medical Officers of the Army of Tennessee," *Southern Historical Society Papers* 22 (1894), 273.

Bevens was officially detached to the Medical Department at this same time, September 1862. From January 1863 through August 1864, he was designated a hospital steward. Service Records, Roll 46.

14. To be "gagged and bucked" was a common punishment for minor infractions of military law in both northern and southern armies. The man was seated on the ground. His hands and feet were bound with his knees drawn up between his arms and a heavy stick thrust under the knees and over the arms. He was than gagged.

15. The army marched due north from Munfordville toward Nolin, Kentucky, on September 20. Just south of Nolin, it veered northeast toward Bardstown.

had no time. He stayed, however, to look on, and embarrassed the young surgeon still more. When Dr. Young took the knife his hand shook like a leaf, but he performed the operation successfully and according to all the laws of surgery. After the war he returned to his home at Corinth, Mississippi, where he stood high in his profession. He died in 1892.[13]

At Munfordville while in the line of battle, marching slowly and stopping often, we passed through an orchard. Nice juicy apples were lying all over the ground and one of the boys of a Louisiana Regiment stooped down and picked up two or three. His colonel happened to be looking in his direction, and he had that boy gagged and bucked everytime the line stopped. After that every soldier thought hell was too good for that colonel.[14]

On the 20th [of September] we marched all night and camped at daylight at New Haven. On the 21st we marched seventeen miles, and camped at Haginsville.[15] On the 22nd we passed fine orchards. My partner, Dr. Arnold said to me, "If you will carry my surplus baggage, I will take the risk and get some of those apples." "Now Pard, you are in for more trouble." But he would not listen, and taking his blanket to hold the apples he started off.

He was not the only soldier under the trees, and while on a limb getting his share of the apples, lo and

16. The First Arkansas arrived at Bardstown on September 23. General Bragg, appreciating their fatigue, reported, "The troops at Bardstown, much jaded and foot-sore from the long and arduous march, were placed in position for rest and recuperation." OR, vol. 16, pt. 1, 1091.

Bevens seems to have been unaware of the confusion in the Confederate high command over the timing of the movement out of Bardstown. The movement finally did come on October 4, but it was in the nature of a retreat eastward toward Danville, away from the Union army positioned north of Bardstown. See McWhiney, *Braxton Bragg,* 299–308; Joseph H. Parks, *General Leonidas Polk, C.S.A.: The Fighting Bishop* (Baton Rouge: Louisiana State University Press, 1962), 262–68; Steven E. Woodworth, *Jefferson Davis and his Generals: The Failure of Confederate Command in the West* (Lawrence: University of Kansas Press, 1990), 155–57.

behold, the provost guard came to arrest them! He fairly fell from the tree, broke through the high corn and ran for his life, the guard calling after, "Halt, or I shoot."

He got back to us with the fruit but said the apples had cost him so much labor and so much fright that they did not taste good. Because we laughed at him, running with his load, he would not give us any until the next day.

We marched fifteen miles and camped at Bardstown until October 4th, when we marched seventeen miles. We marched twelve miles and camped at Springfield. The heat was terrible on those long sunny pikes, with never a sign to mark the grave of a hero, noble sacrifice to their cause.[16]

One day an assistant surgeon carrying an umbrella was marching along the pike in the rear of his regiment when General Hardee came along. The General had nothing to shield him from the sun but a little cap. He rode up to the surgeon and said, "What is your name?"

The man told him his name, rank and regiment.

"Well sir," said General Hardee, "just imagine this whole army with umbrellas."

The doctor shut up his umbrella and pitched it over into the field.

General Hardee was always joking his men on the

17. General Anderson's division camped at Salt River, between Perryville and Harrodsburg, on the night of October 6. Connelly, *Army of the Heartland*, 256.

18. Bevens writes elsewhere of the thirst of men at Perryville and the importance of the spring. "Men were dying [of thirst]." he recalled. *Confederate Veteran* 28 (February 1920), 70.

march, but when the fight was on no one did his part better than he.

On October 6th we marched through Perryville, but on the 7th we marched back and camped in the main street of the town.[17]

Some of the boys stole a bee-hive and many of them got stung so their faces were swollen and eyes closed. Dr. Arnold was one of the injured ones, but he did not fail to eat his honey. As we lay on the ground that night I teased him, saying General Hardee would need no further proof; that he carried his guilt on his face. The doctor did not relish this so I turned over to go to sleep when a bee stung me on the cheek.

"Who's the guilty one now?" laughed the doctor and the joke was surely on me. But I knew where the medicine wagon was, and went and got some ammonia. I bathed my face, and the swelling went down at once, so I came out ahead after all.

By daylight we were in the line of battle and honey and bee-stings were forgotten. The Battle of Perryville was fought October 8th, 1862. We were on the extreme left and our battery, on a hill at our rear, was not engaged until late in the day. The heaviest fighting was on the extreme right. Both sides were contending stubbornly for a spring of water between the lines and were dying for water.[18]

19. General Hardee commanded the left wing of the army at Perryville; Colonel Powell's brigade and the Louisiana Brigade of Brig. Gen. Daniel Weisiger Adams "covered the extreme left" of Hardee's line. But the First Arkansas was never committed to battle, and so saw only the limited action described by Bevens. OR, vol. 16, pt. 1, 111–12, 1121–22. One historian says the Confederate left was extremely weak, and when General Adams and Colonel Powell encountered an entire Union corps on their front, they fell back through Perryville. Connelly, *Army of the Heartland*, 266. Casualties at Perryville were 4,211 (of 37,000) Federals, 3,396 (of 16,000) Confederates.

20. Bevens is slightly off on the itinerary of the withdrawal from Perryville. Bragg halted his forces at Harrodsburg, about ten miles northeast of Perryville, on October 10. He then marched fifteen miles eastward to Bryantsville, where he arrived on October 11. McWhiney, *Braxton Bragg*, 320–21. Camp Robinson had been established by the Federals as a training camp for Kentucky recruits about five miles south of Bryantsville. The "council" Bevens mentions convened on October 12 at Bryantsville and involved Bragg, Kirby Smith, Hardee, and generals Leonidas Polk, Benjamin Franklin Cheatham, and Humphrey Marshall. It was decided to withdraw from Kentucky back into Tennessee. The next day, the army headed for Cumberland Gap.

Sometimes one side would have the advantage, sometimes the other. When called into action we crossed a bridge in the center of the town, formed a line and advanced to the top of the hill. Our battery was planted and had begun its work when we received orders to recross the bridge and occupy our former lines. We had to retreat under battery fire, and after we had got our battery over the bridge we marched along the pike. The enemy opened on us with grape and canister and did deadly work. We double-quicked into line and their sharpshooters gave us a terrible assault from behind the houses. But when our line was formed, our sharpshooters deployed and our battery opened fire, they had to retreat. So the battle went on, but finally we had to give up the struggle and evacuate the town. The loss was heavy on both sides, about eight thousand men being killed, captured and wounded.[19]

October 9th we marched fifteen miles and passed Harrodsburg. On the 10th we marched sixteen miles to Camp Dick Robinson. Here a council was held while General Bragg gave his wagons time to go South. It was the greatest wagon train ever seen in the army; was three days passing at one point. Here George Thomas and I each bought three yards of undyed jeans to make ourselves some trousers when we got back South.[20]

21. The Confederate attack on
Richmond, Kentucky, by forces
under Kirby Smith and the ensuing
engagement occurred on August
29–30, 1862. The Federals lost
5,353 of 6,500 troops, the great
bulk of them being captured. The
Confederates lost only 451 of 6,850
men.

The defeat at Perryville and the failure of the Kentuckians to join us as we had hoped, made our campaign anything but a brilliant success from a military point of view, notwithstanding our victories at Munfordville and Richmond.[21]

But we had captured six thousand men, we had secured arms and ammunition which were sorely needed, we had gotten enormous quantities of supplies which were a great help to the Confederacy, and the men who did get back were tough as whitleather, ready for anything.

October 13th we marched twenty-three miles, passing through Lancaster. October 14th we marched seventeen miles, going through Mount Vernon, and halted a little before dark.

Dr. Arnold and I went down to a creek about a mile from camp, and there in a field we found a fine pumpkin. He said if I would help him cook it I might help him eat it. He said it would have to cook until one o'clock to be well done. I told him I would help take it to camp but I'd be dinged if I'd stay up until one o'clock to cook it. I was too nearly dead for rest and sleep. We got it to camp, cut it up, put it in the famous old army camp kettle and Doc began the Herculean task of staying awake to cook his pumpkin. He did stay awake until one o'clock and got it nicely done, but was afraid to eat it at that unusual

22. Skirmishing occurred at or near Wild Cat, Kentucky, October 17–20, 1862, but there is no evidence that Maj. Gen. Simon Bolivar Buckner participated. A year earlier, October 21, 1861, a larger engagement occurred at Camp Wild Cat, or Rockcastle Hills. Buckner was in Kentucky at the time, but he was commanding forces at Bowling Green.

23. "Jayhawkers" was a term applied to Unionists sympathizers and guerrillas. Eastern Tennessee was notorious for its anti-Confederate sentiment.

hour, as he might have cramp colic. He found an old fashioned oven with a lid, put his pumpkin into it, fastened the lid, placed the oven under the knapsack beneath his head and went to sleep. But first he took the trouble to wake me and tell me I should not have a bite of his pumpkin because I would not stay up to help him cook it.

When reveille sounded he woke up and began to guy me, saying "You shall not have a bite." He took up his knapsack and behold, the oven, pumpkin and all, was gone! Oh, he was furious, and fairly pawed the ground. He thought I had taken it for a joke, but soon found that to be a mistake. We decided that some soldier had stolen and eaten it. If he had found the man he would have fought him to a finish. He never did see the joke.

October 19th we marched eleven miles. We passed over a battlefield, where General Buckner had fought, and crossed Wild Cat River.[22] We marched thirteen miles and passed through Barkersville. This was a strong Union town in the the mountains. The "Jay Hawkers" shot at us from the top of the mountains; women and boys pelted us with stones, shouting, "Hurrah, for the Union." As they were women and children, we had to take it.[23]

Once we were marching on a road cut out of the mountain side. On one side was a cliff of solid rock,

24. Another instance of Hardee's concern for his men, especially the sick and wounded, was recorded by a soldier who recalled how the general would sometimes "give up his horse to some barefooted or sick soldier and walk for miles." Quoted in McWhiney, *Braxton Bragg,* 276.

on the other a deep precipice. The command to halt was given and the men fell down to rest, completely filling the road. Arnold and I were in the rear, and one of the ambulance drivers, seeing the crowded condition of the road, told us to get up with him, which we did. There was a trail just wide enough for the horsemen, single file, and along this trail rode General Hardee looking after his men. When he reached this ambulance he stopped opposite Arnold and said to him, "Are you sick?" "No sir." "Well, get down off that wagon."

"Are you sick?" he called to me, but by that time I was out on the ground. Then he said to the driver, "Let no soldier ride unless he is sick or wounded."

A Kentucky Colonel brought with him his five hundred dollar carriage, and had his negro drive it at the rear of the regiment. In his rounds General Hardee had found some sick men and told them to get into that carriage. The negro and rear officers explained whose carriage it was, but the General only said, "No use going empty when it can serve so good a purpose. By tomorrow perhaps none of us will need it."

So the umbrella man, Arnold and myself were not the only ones upon whom General Hardee kept an eye.[24]

October 19th we marched fourteen miles, crossed

25. The "creeping enemy" referred to by Bevens were the lice, fleas, and other vermin that infested the clothes of soldiers on campaign. Bevens does not seem to recall, however, a heavy snow that fell the night of October 25, in Knoxville. The accompanying cold should have provided some relief from the insects. See Ted R. Worley, ed., *They Never Came Back: The War Memoirs of Captain John W. Lavender, C.S.A.* (Pine Bluff, Ark.: Southern Press, 1956), 33.

26. T. R. Ashford was appointed assistant surgeon July 1862. His first recorded appointment was to the Thirty-first Arkansas Infantry in December 1862. Later he served with the Second Tennessee Infantry. Jones, "Roster of the Medical Officers of the Army of Tennessee," 169.

A Tennessee soldier on the same march from Kentucky to Knoxville said that his company "got very thirsty for tobacco." For their solution to the emergency see Sam R. Watkins, *"Co. Aytch": A Side Show of the Big Show* (New York: Collier Books, 1962), 71–72.

Cumberland River, then on through Gibralter, Cumberland Gap, and on across Powell River into Tennessee. We marched past Tazewell, crossed Clinch River at Madisonville, and, on October 24th, camped about six miles from Knoxville. Here we were given time to wash and dry our clothes. On this raid we had only one suit and to get it clean meant to strip, wash, let the clothes dry on or hang them on bushes to dry, while we waited. With our battles and forced marches we could not stop for that; so creeping companions were large and furious, and made deadly war. But at Knoxville everybody got busy, went into warfare with our creeping enemy, and the thousands destroyed in that fierce combat will never be known.[25]

George Thomas and I brought out our white jeans which we had bought in camp Dick Robinson, and had carried all these miles. We got some copperas from a kind old rebel lady, took walnut hulls and dyed our cloth. It was a good job too.

The boys were getting short on tobacco, and it looked as if the whole army would be forced to reform on this line. But they borrowed Dr. Ashford's horse and sent me to buy tobacco, chewing tobacco, smoking tobacco, hand tobacco, giving me plenty of Confederate currency.[26]

I rode into the beautiful town which I had not

27. General Bragg was not the
brigade commander; that would
have been Colonel Powell.

seen since we were flying into Virginia. Then we wore good clothes and had Sunday Soldiering. Now we were soldiers with the dust of a thousand mile march, ragged and unkempt, bleeding from the wounds of two hard-fought battles and numerous skirmishes. Then we were raw, undisciplined troops, now we were seasoned veterans. Such was the change in a few short months.

Riding to a drug store, I hitched my horse, went in, and bought my wholesale bill of tobacco. When I came out again to the sidewalk I saw a policeman leading off my horse. I yelled at him to stop, but he went on. I rushed up and grabbed the reins. He told me it was against the law to hitch a horse to a post in that city. About that time twenty of our boys came running to my rescue. They lined up and told the policeman to turn the horse loose. He did the wise thing, or there would have been a "hot time" right there. I took the horse and made a bee-line for General Bragg's Brigade, and took joy and delight to my tobacco-starving friends.[27]

November 2nd we passed through Knoxville and camped on the railroad. At daylight the 154th Regiment Band awoke us with the sweetest music I ever heard. It brought back such poignant memories of home, of the boys and girls around the piano, of charming plantation melodies.

28. The East Tennessee and Georgia Railroad carried the army to Chattanooga; the Nashville and Chattanooga Railroad carried it from there to Bridgeport, about twenty-five miles west and slightly south of Chattanooga. Bragg moved his headquarters from Chattanooga on November 12 and had established himself at Tullahoma, Tennessee, by November 14. On November 20, the Army of the Mississippi became the Army of Tennessee, and the inevitable reorganization followed, although the First Arkansas was not immediately affected. OR, vol. 20, pt. 2, 400, 402, 411, 419–20.

But the next tune was not so sweet. It came to the tune of orders to "cook three days' rations, and be ready to move at a moment's notice." We rode cars to Chattanooga, from there on November 10th we went to Bridgeport, Alabama. From Bridgeport we crossed the Tennessee River, marched fifty miles and camped at Alisonia. November 24th we marched twenty miles, passing through Tullahoma; November 25th we marched fifteen miles and camped on Duck River at a short distance from Shelbyville.[28] At this time the Medical department decided to give all the one-course Medical students then in the army a chance to pass the examination for promotion to assistant surgeon. Dr. Arnold was one of these one-course students and decided to try the examination. We diked him out in the best clothes we could get together in the company. I contributed my white shirt, other boys brought him hat, coat, shoes, and collar. When he stood before us for inspection he could have passed for a lawyer or preacher just from town. With his book, "Smith's Compends," he walked twenty miles to the Board of Examiners, stood before the "saw-bones," shook and answered questions. Perhaps his borrowed plumage helped him, at any rate he passed, and was given a certificate. He walked back, changed from the rank of a private to

29. Arnold passed his medical board examination for assistant surgeon on November 26, 1982. Jones, "Roster of the Medical Officers of the Army of Tennessee," 169. His book, Smith's "Compends," was a widely used medical textbook of the day by Francis Gurney Smith and John Neill, *An Analytical Compendium of the Various Branches of Medical Service, for the Use and Examination of Students* (Philadelphia: Lea and Blanchard, 1848). The stated purpose of the Confederate medical board examination was to "scrutinize rigidly the moral habits, professional acquirements, and physical qualifications of the candidates, and report favorably, either for appointment or promotion, in no case admitting of reasonable doubt." Contemporary reports on the difficulty of passing the examination are mixed. Some people thought it was ridiculously easy, but the majority consensus seems to have been that the boards performed their mission admirably. H. H. Cunningham, *Doctors in Gray: The Confederate Medical Service* (Baton Rouge: Louisiana State University Press, 1958), 32–35.

30. General Hardee received orders to march his corps from Shelbyville to Eagleville, twenty-two miles to the north, on December 4. The army settled in around College Grove, near Eagleville, about twenty miles west of Murfreesboro. On December 12,

General Anderson's division, which had escaped reorganization in November, was now disbanded. The First Arkansas, still commanded by Colonel Colquitt, remained in Hardee's corps, but it now served in Maj. Gen. Patrick Ronayne Cleburne's Second Division, and in that division's First Brigade, commanded by Brig. Gen. Lucius Eugene Polk. Also in Polk's brigade were the Thirteenth and Fifteenth Arkansas (Consolidated), Fifth Confederate, Second Tennessee, Fifth Tennessee, and Calvert's (or Helena) Arkansas Battery. OR, vol. 20, pt. 2, 439, 448–49.

31. In the battle of Stones River, or Murfreesboro (December 31, 1862–January 3, 1863), Maj. Gen. William Starke Rosecrans (1819–1902) led his Army of the Cumberland out of Nashville to face Bragg. The First Arkansas moved into line of battle on December 30, only to sit and wait through the night for the dawn attack. When Cleburne's division finally moved forward, it formed the army's second line, behind Maj. Gen. John Porter McCown's division, on the left of Bragg's army. Polk's brigade was positioned third in line from the left within the division, and the First Arkansas was placed second from the left within the brigade. Peter Cozzens, *No Better Place to Die: The Battle of Stones River* (Urbana: University of Illinois Press, 1990), 84.

that of a captain! When he came in sight two hundred braves met him; when shown his certificate they rode him on a rail and kept up a rough house for an hour or two. He had no horse, no money, and no books except his Smith's Compends, but the older doctors helped him, and soon he was fully up in medical affairs and made a good surgeon too.[29]

December 8th we marched twenty miles and camped at Eaglesville. From there we marched to College Hill.[30]

December 28th we marched to Murfreesboro, and camped on Stones River within cannon shot of the town. Here we prepared to meet Rosecrans with his army, forty-five thousand in number. We were in line of battle on the extreme right. After dark on the thirtieth, still in line of battle, we moved our position to extreme left and camped, without fire, in a cedar rough. Our orders were to advance as soon as it was light enough to see. At dawn, December 31, we moved promptly on the enemy, advancing through an open field. The enemy, protected by a fence and the trees, received us with deadly fire and our loss was great. But we flew after them and our work was just as disastrous to them. Dead bluecoats were thick in every direction. We soon had them on the run.[31]

Our company Color Bearer William Mathews, the same who had defied the Yankee fleet on the

32. Mathews was so badly wounded that he spent the better part of a year in military hospitals at Newman and Forsyth, Georgia. Service Records, Roll 49.

33. Sergeant Thomas was wounded "slightly" in the hip and arm. He spent several weeks in a military hospital at Rome, Georgia. Service Records, Roll 52.

34. Arthur P. Green, a private in Company G, was born in Virginia about 1837. According to the census of 1860, he worked as a blacksmith and lived with his mother, Mary P. Green, and two younger sisters. His mother was an English-born schoolteacher. Left for dead on the battlefield, Green was taken prisoner and died January 2, 1863, at Murfreesboro while in Federal hands. As a result of his sacrifice, Green was named to the army's Roll of Honor. Service Records, Roll 48. The Roll of Honor was enacted by the Confederate Congress in October 1862 to recognize soldiers "conspicuous for courage and good conduct on the field of battle" in lieu of "medals and badges of distinction." Fifteen members of the First Arkansas received this signal honor following the fighting at Stones River. OR, vol. 20, pt. 1, 972–74; Hammock, *With Honor Untarnished*, 81.

Potomac, had been ill and this was his first fight. As we followed the fleeing Yanks he said, "Boys, this is fun." One of the men answered, "Stripes, don't be so quick, this is not over yet; you may get a ninety-day furlough yet." In twenty minutes Mathews' arm was shot to pieces.[32]

George Thomas was in front of all the company. He had killed two men and was pulling down on the third, when one, but a short distance away, shot him, wounding him in the arm. But George spotted the man who shot him and wanted to go on with one good arm. However, he was taken off the field and sent to the hospital.[33]

We drove the enemy three miles. The fire all along the line was terrific. The cannonading could be heard for miles. The rattle of small arms was continuous. Our line on the left was pressing on over a terrible cedar rough. Anyone who understands a cedar rough can understand what that means. Limestone rocks, gnarly cedar trees, stub arms sticking out of the ground, make it almost impassable at best. How much more difficult with an enemy in front concentrating his fire upon us. We pressed on through rocks and thicket. One of our brave boys, Arthur Green, was struck by a cannonball and torn all to pieces.[34] Other parts of the line were as hot as ours. We got possession of the thicket but could not get the

35. What made the firing particularly heavy was the fact that the First Arkansas had pursued so vigorously that, as at Shiloh, the regiment found itself subject to enfilading fire from Federal batteries. Bevens neglects to mention that a portion of the regiment, along with the Fifth Confederate, captured several Union cannon in the advance. General Cleburne reinforces Bevens's opinion of the difficulty of advancing through a cedar brake: "I found the enemy had made another stand in a heavy cedar brake. . . . He had again found natural breastworks of limestone rock, and covered most of his line behind them. He made an obstinate and destructive resistance, during which Polk's brigade suffered a severe repulse; but he was finally dislodged and driven from the cedars." OR, vol. 20, pt. 1, 844–46, 853. Pvt. Samuel H. Williams, of Company I, was impressed by a variety of very mixed images during this phase of the battle. On the one hand, he distinctly recalled a flock of wild turkeys, too frightened to fly, running "helter-skelter" between the lines. Likewise, innumerable rabbits raced "hither and thither," although many of these small creatures "were trampled to death in the melee." On the other hand, he also recalled a member of his company being "literally cut in two by a cannon ball. . . . I saw men wounded in every manner imaginable," he elaborated. "Some with their noses shot off, some with their fingers and toes shot away. I saw one poor fellow with both legs severed by a cannon ball." *Washington* [Arkansas] *Telegraph,* 25 February 1863, 2.

Before advancing out of the cedars, Cleburne reformed his lines. This resulted in Polk's brigade being placed on the extreme right of the division, although the First Arkansas maintained its place in the brigade's formation. At this "critical moment" in the battle, at about 1 P.M., the division moved against a fresh Union line that had been reinforced by artillery. The heavy fire and a belief that they were about to be outflanked caused the men to falter. "As our broken ranks went back over the fields before the edge of this fresh line," Cleburne reported, "the enemy opened fire on our right flank, inflicting a heavier loss on Polk's brigade than it had suffered in all the previous fighting of the day." The division fell back about four hundred yards to reform and be resupplied with ammunition and to await a counterattack that never came. And just as well, for Polk's men were exhausted. They had been fighting and advancing by this time for seven hours. "My men at the time they were repulsed," Polk reported, "were much jaded, having been fighting since early in the morning, without any rest, and had nearly exhausted their ammunition." Cozzens, *No Better Place to Die,* 147; OR, vol. 20, pt. 1, 847–49, 854.

cannon through it; so we hardly got a man of their line.

When we got through, we found the Yanks with sixty cannon in line fronting the cedar rough. Our ranks were so depleted we could not charge two lines of infantry and sixty cannon. There was nothing to do but hold our position and await re-inforcements.[35]

We lay in line all night. Orders were sent to the quarter-master to send rations, if he had any. Two negroes, belonging to two of the officers, arrived, bringing food for their masters.

As all was quiet then, and it was raining, they decided to sleep by the fire until daylight. To keep off the rain they drove forked branches into the ground, laid a brace across them, stretched their blankets over all, and pegged them to the ground at the four corners. Before long hard firing was heard on the outpost. Bullets rained on their tent, struck the logs of the fire, cut loose the corners of the blankets, letting the rain on their faces. When they saw the flying bullets, they awaited no instructions from their masters. With eyes popping out of their heads, they grabbed their blankets and set out for the wagon train. They were not long in getting there.

Next day the struggle was renewed with fearful carnage.

Each side fought with grim and settled purpose, finally a fierce onslaught scattered our forces. In

36. Bevens forgets that no heavy fighting occurred on January 1, and, indeed, the regiment was not seriously tested again, although it held its position for two more days. Heavy skirmishing continued on the division's front "night and day," but after a last concerted Federal effort to break the line on the night of January 2, Polk's brigade was ordered back to its position of December 30. On January 3, Bragg's army withdrew. OR, vol. 20, pt. 1, 854. Elsewhere Bevens recalled of Stones River: "It was bitter cold, sleeting and raining, and to watch the old year out and the new year in with no tents over your head and Rosecrans' army in front of you was not the most desirable thing in the world." *Confederate Veteran* 28 (February 1920), 70.

37. Bevens's estimate of casualties is essentially correct. The Federals lost 12,906 of 41,400 men; the Confederates lost 11,739 of 34,739 men. Polk's brigade lost 337; the First Arkansas, 102. OR, vol. 20, pt. 1, 680.

38. Donelson McGregor, born about 1831 in Tennessee, was a relative of Andrew Jackson. The 1860 census listed McGregor as a Jefferson County farmer worth $12,350, but that was a modest sum compared to the fortune of the relative with whom he lived, Flowers McGregor, who owned $100,000 in land and almost $50,000 in personal property. McGregor marched off to war as the captain of Clan McGregor, from Pine Bluff, Jefferson County. This unit became Company D in the First Arkansas. While at Tupelo, Colonel Colquitt had made McGregor his chief of staff.

twenty minutes we lost two thousand men, and the day was lost. Orders for retreat were given.[36]

General Bragg's loss was about ten thousand men, while Rosecrans reported his at twelve thousand.[37]

In the battle our Lieutenant Colonel Don McGregor was mortally wounded. When he was taken to the hospital, his faithful old Samuel was by his side. The Colonel's sister, who lived a few miles from Murfreesboro, had come to relieve the suffering and nurse the wounded. (Ah, those brave, never-to-be-forgotten daughters of the South!) When she drove up to the hospital in her carriage she found Sam waiting with his own and his master's horse saddled ready for the trip to her home. When we retreated General Rosecrans' men came in, and his guard took the two horses, and drove off in the carriage. What could be done? Samuel said, "I will get them back."[38]

At this particular time of the unpleasantness, the Yankees were burning with sympathy for the poor, oppressed negro, and negroes were permitted to do pretty much as they pleased. Samuel went to Rosecrans' headquarters, told him the horses were his, that he had a wounded friend in the hospital and he wanted a pass to the country. All his requests were granted. He drove the Colonel and his sister to her home, and nursed his master until he died.

39. General Hardee's adjutant was
Lt. Col. Thomas B. Roy.

After Colonel McGregor died Samuel got a pass through the lines and returned to our camp. He delivered the Colonel's horse but kept his own and asked our Regiment Colonel for a pass to Arkansas. He then told the boys to write to their fathers, mothers and sweethearts, as he was going back home to see his mistress. We received answers to these letters, showing that Samuel had made the journey safely, faithful to the end.

We retreated by night. We were nearly starved. It was raining, cold, cold rain, and we were wet to the skin. We were so sleepy that if we stopped for a moment we would go to sleep. We had gone almost as far as human nature could go.

One of the boys thought he would rest a few moments beside a fire left by some wagons. He took pine boughs and laid them on the wet ground, dropped down with all his accoutrements, and went to sleep. General Hardee came up, spied him, called to his Adjutant, "Roy, come here; here is a fellow who has gone regularly to bed."[39]

About then the soldier woke up very much frightened. He thought he would be shot. He got away from there in a hurry, and was with his command before his absence was discovered.

January 5th, 1863, we marched forty-two miles to Manchester. January 6th we marched eighteen miles

40. General Hardee, author of the famous drill manual, *Rifle and Light Infantry Tactics,* 2 vols. (Philadelphia: Lippincott, Grambo, & Company, 1855), had a reputation for drilling his men relentlessly. At Tullahoma, his corps (not his "Division") drilled and practiced maneuvers hour after hour, with frequent inspections by Hardee himself. General Cleburne, the division commander, was also a stickler for drill at the Tullahoma camp. Nathaniel C. Hughes, Jr., *General William J. Hardee, Old Reliable* (Baton Rouge: Louisiana State University Press, 1965), 151; Howell and Elizabeth Purdue, *Pat Cleburne, Confederate General* (Hillsboro, Tex.: Hill Junior College Press, 1973), 185–86.

41. "Town ball" was an early form of baseball. "Bull pen" was a game (known also as "Bull in the ring" and "Wild bull") in which players join hands and form a ring around a "bull" who tries to break through the ring. If he escapes, the other players chase him. Whoever catches him becomes the new "bull." Elsewhere, Bevens says Bill Barnes "was something of a musical genius, and could play any kind of instrument." Indeed, Barnes was so good a musician that in 1863 he was detailed to the division band at General Cleburne's headquarters. William E. Bevens, "Makers of Jackson County: Short Stories of Early Pioneers, and Something about the Founding of Old Jacksonport," eds.

Lady Elizabeth Luker and James Logan Morgan, *Stream of History* 21 (March 1984), 11–12.

42. On April 15, a captain in Hardee's corps informed his brother, "The troops are in good spirits, and are confident of success when an engagement takes place, and, if the weather continues good, we expect it soon." OR, vol. 23, pt. 2, 773. However, while Company G may have been feeling fit in the spring of 1863, some soldiers' families were feeling the pinch of war. The county court had first considered the need for relief of soldiers' families in July 1861, when it authorized $500 for that purpose. In December 1862, the Arkansas legislature also approved relief funds. Jackson County received $6,360 of these funds in March 1863. At least 208 Jackson County families applied for relief, and by June 1863 all but $74 of a total fund of $6,750 had been allocated. Four families of Company G are known to have applied for relief: Daniel Hays (who had been killed), Owen L. Slaughter, Alfred Stewart, and Daniel Boone Winningham. Watson, *Fight and Survive!,* 12–16, 54–55; Lady Elizabeth Luker, "List of Confederate Soldiers Found in Old Ledger," *Stream of History* 5 (April 1967), 23–30; James Logan Morgan, *Families of Confederate Soldiers of Jackson County, Arkansas, 1861–1863* (Newport, Ark.: Morgan Books, 1982), 1, 5–6, 20, 30, 31, 34.

to Alisonia. From Alisonia we marched to Tullahoma, and there we camped for the winter.

We were in General Hardee's Division. We had tents and were comfortable. We drilled four hours a day, and by way of diversion General Hardee had contests in drilling. We became so expert that we could have made the Virginia Cadets ashamed of themselves. Our company was third best and that took good practice.[40] A Louisiana company was ahead of us. It beat us in quickness at "trail arms", "lie down", at "double-quick." At walking or running none excelled us at any army maneuver. We had other amusements, too. We played "town ball" and "bull pen" and had some lively games. We dressed up the smaller fellows as girls and we danced. Joe Hamilton, Dick Haden, Sam Shoup and Bill Barnes were the musicians.[41] Bill Shackleford was ready to play pranks, and made fun for the crowd. Now and then we got a pass and sent our best foragers out for "fancy grub" and vegetables. Then we would have a big dinner and a big day.

April 23rd, real fun began again, but we were alive, active, young, healthy, well-drilled, well disciplined—in perfect fighting trim.[42] For fear we would forget how to march a walking track was opened up from Tullahoma, and we marched daily five, ten, eighteen, twenty, thirty miles, making expeditions to

43. Hardee's corps was transferred to Wartrace, Tennessee, about twenty miles northwest of Tullahoma, to protect the Nashville and Chattanooga Railroad against a potential Union advance. From there, as Bevens suggests, Hardee regularly sent out pickets and even whole brigades on expeditions to surrounding towns as a show of force against Rosecrans' army, which had wintered at Murfreesboro. A member of Company E complained in mid-June that the regiment had been marching for three solid weeks, never staying more than three days in any one place. "I never was so tired of moving in my life," he wrote from Manchester. He admitted that there were lots of pretty girls in that part of the country, but if they were going to be marched to death, he preferred that the regiment be sent to help break the Union siege of Vicksburg. "I think us Arks boys would fight mighty hard, to keep them from cutting off Communication between us and Arks," he told a cousin. "I think the Feds are playing out pretty fast, if we can hold Vicksburg all is saved." Hughes, *General William J. Hardee*, 154–55; Frederick W. Bush to Emily, 19 June 1863, Frederick W. Bush Letters, Special Collections, University of Arkansas Library.

At Wartrace, the troops became a bit rowdy, especially in their search for building materials for shelters. Hardee issued a general order dated April 25 in which he warned his men to stay on good terms with civilians and especially to "respect the rights and property of citizens, whose labors are necessary to the subsistence of our armies." On that same day, Hardee wrote from Wartrace, "My entire corps is now in position. . . . We are all delighted with the change to this position. The country is beautiful and rich in pastures." OR, vol. 23, pt. 2, 790–91, 796–97, 813, 827, 849, 851–52, 884, 888–89.

44. I have been unable to identify the Louisiana regiment referred to by Bevens. The only Louisiana infantry in Bragg's army were the Thirteenth and Twentieth Louisiana (Consolidated), Sixteenth and Twenty-fifth Louisiana (Consolidated), and Fourteenth Louisiana Battalion. All were in Col. Randall L. Gibson's brigade of Maj. Gen. John C. Breckinridge's division. Additionally, the Nineteenth Louisiana joined the army at Tullahoma in April from Mobile. But all of these units had fought at Stones River, and all had been transferred to Mississippi in May. Following reorganization of the army in July, the only remaining Louisiana infantry in the entire army was the First Louisiana, which formed part of the artillery reserve. See Arthur W. Bergeron, Jr., *Guide to Louisiana Confederate Military Units 1861–1865* (Baton Rouge: Louisiana State University Press, 1989), 69–71, 102–106, 112–15, 120–22, 167–68.

all the surrounding towns—Wartrace, Bellbuckle, Hoover's Gap, Duck River, Bridge, Railroad Gap, Manchester.[43] Manchester was a nice little town in the hills, where there were numerous springs and streams in which we could swim. June 22nd we went there to relieve a Louisiana Regiment. When we arrived they were on dress parade, eleven hundred strong and their drill was simply fine, but they had never smelt powder nor marched at all. They wore nice caps, fine uniforms, white gloves, fine shop-made laced high shoes. They carried fat haversacks and new canteens, fine new fat knapsacks with lots of underclothing and even two pairs of shoes. They laughed at us in our shabby dress, with our dirty haversacks and no knapsacks. We had one suit of underwear wrapped in our blankets and our accoutrements were reduced to the lightest weight possible. They said we were too few to meet the enemy, but we told them we would stay with any who came to engage us. We also told them that they couldn't get through one week's campaign with such knapsacks. Some of the boys said, "We will follow in your wake and replenish our wardrobes."[44]

This was a sad camp to us. One of our men, Garrett, got angry with Mr. Brogden, the Beef Sergeant, who divided the company rations. Taking his gun, he went to Brogden's tent where he was

45. Pvt. James C. Garrett killed Theophilus H. Brogden on June 22, 1863. According to the census of 1860, Brogden was born in North Carolina about 1826. He worked as a carpenter in Prairie County, Arkansas. Interestingly, one of the three other men with whom he lived before the war—all bachelors and all carpenters or plasterers—was W. S. Garrett. James C. Garrett, who lived in Jackson County, was born about 1840 and worked as a cook. His service record shows that he was absent from the regiment after July 1863. Service Records, Rolls 46–47.

46. Bevens seems to be in error when he says the regiment advanced to Wartrace from Manchester on these dates. Although it is logical that if at Manchester the regiment would have left on June 27 (Rosecrans was there by June 28), General Cleburne's report says that General Polk's entire brigade was at Tullahoma on June 24. He does mention evacuating some

troops at or near Wartrace to Tullahoma on June 27, but, in the absence of reports by Polk or his regimental commanders, it is difficult to pinpoint the First Arkansas's position. OR, vol. 23, pt. 1, 586–87; Hughes, *General William J. Hardee,* 156–57; Purdue, *Pat Cleburne,* 192–93.

Bevens fails to explain that the army's movements were necessary because Rosecrans' Army of the Cumberland was in hot pursuit. This is the Tullahoma Campaign (June 23–30), which culminated in the evacuation of Tullahoma by the Confederates.

47. Gen. Leonidas Polk and Rev. Charles T. Quintard founded the University of the South at Sewanee, Tennessee, in 1860. The retreat into the Cumberland Mountains became necessary when Rosecrans' army gained control of the Elk River. Bragg now intended to head for the Tennessee River, cross it, and make his stand. OR, vol. 23, pt. 1, 584.

unarmed and shot him like a dog. Garrett would have been lynched if the officers had not hurried him off to another part of the army.[45]

June 27th we marched to Wartrace, June 29th to Tullahoma, June 30th we were deployed to build breastworks, but we retreated at eleven o'clock at night to Alisonia on Elk River.[46]

July third, we camped in the Cumberland Mountains, near the school which had been established by General Polk and the Quintards. It was an ideal place for a school and I am glad to say it bears, today, an honored name among educators as the University of the South.[47]

We had marched all day in the hot July sun, clouds of dust had parched our throats, and we were almost perishing for water when we reached the spring. As we rested at the side of the road whom should we see but our crack Louisiana Regiment—the one we had relieved at Manchester only ten days before. They were dusty, dirty, lame and halt, with feet sore and swollen in their tight shoes, a bedraggled and woe begone set of youngsters. How we joshed them.

"Don't cry, mama's darling;" "Straighten up and be men;" "Brace up like soldiers, so the army won't be ashamed of you." These were some of the commands we hurled at them. They would have fought us if they could have stopped, but a soldier cannot break ranks.

48. The crossing of the Tennessee River at Kelly's Ford occurred on July 6–7. Tyner's Station is about eight miles east of Chattanooga on the East Tennessee and Georgia Railroad. Cleburne's division was assigned to guard the upriver fords of the Tennessee River east of Chattanooga. Again, Bevens gives no indication that the army was continuing to retreat before Rosecrans. During the weeks at Tyner's Station, General Cleburne kept the men busy by drilling them and having them construct rifle pits and four forts in and near Tyner's Station. Purdue, *Pat Cleburne,* 195–56, 203–204.

On July 31, before leaving Tyner's Station, another reorganization of the Army of Tennessee found the First Arkansas with a new corps commander: Lt. Gen. Daniel Harvey Hill. General Polk's brigade now consisted of the First Arkansas, Third and Fifth Confederate (Consolidated), Second Tennessee, Thirty-fifth Tennessee, Forty-eighth Tennessee, and Calvert's Battery. OR, vol. 23, pt. 2, 942.

49. Graysville, Georgia, is six miles south of Tyner's Station on the Western and Atlantic Railroad.

50. The move to Harrison, twelve miles north of Graysville, was the first northerly movement made by the regiment in some time. Gardner's Ferry should be Gardenshire's Ferry, about twelve miles above Harrison. Rosecrans' army, still north of the Tennessee River, began to threaten several river crossings by mid-August. While a portion of Polk's brigade, commanded by Col. William J. Hill, moved to Gardenshire's Ferry, another portion was rushed to Thatcher's Ferry, south of Harrison. Company G received some much-needed clothing before leaving this region, including ten pairs of shoes, eighteen pairs of drawers, eleven pairs of pants, and eleven shirts. Requisition order in Captain Shoup's file, Service Records, Roll 51.

July 4th, 1863, we camped in the valley on the Tennessee River. Then we crossed the River at Kelly Ford to Lookout Valley. July 9th we marched through Chattanooga and camped at Tyner's Station.[48]

August 17th we marched to Graysville.[49] Here Dr. T. R. Ashford got a four days' furlough. Dr. Ashford had married in Georgia and had gone with his bride to Arkansas and established himself as a physician. When the war broke out he joined the army from his adopted home, going out as assistant surgeon in our regiment. His wife returned to her mother in Georgia and he had not seen her for two years. As Graysville was near her home, she came to visit him and there they had a happy meeting.

Dr. Ashford, always kind and sympathetic, was a great favorite with the boys. Highly educated and a fine surgeon, he was modest and unassuming, a sincere Christian gentleman. After the war he settled in Georgia. Dr. Ashford, Dr. Arnold and I were close friends through those long dreadful years.

August 21st we camped at Harrison on the Tennessee River. On August 23rd we marched fourteen miles and camped at Gardner's Ferry.[50]

Here several of the boys went foraging and got some nice green apples. George Thomas, Captain Shoup and others made apple dumplings and put them in a large camp kettle to cook.

51. This bombardment may have occurred on August 26. One company commander at the Ferry reported that his men were "shelled in [their] Camps from the enemy's guns on the opposite side of the river." Quoted in Purdue, *Pat Cleburne*, 206. A Federal report for that day also mentions bombarding Thatcher's Ferry with "a section of artillery." OR, vol. 30, pt. 3, 176.

The reference to "globe-sighting 16 shotguns" is puzzling. It is descriptive of no known artillery in the war. The rapid-fire Gatling gun had six barrels and six cam-operated bolts that were fired alternately by turning a crank, but the Federals had no such weapons along the Tennessee River. For reference see James C. Hazlett, et al., *Field Artillery Weapons of the Civil War*, 2d ed. (Newark: University of Delaware Press, 1988); Jack Coggins, *Arms and Equipment of the Civil War* (New York: Fairfax Press, 1983), 43–45.

They were standing around the fire, with mouths watering, thinking every minute an hour, when the Yankees on the other side of the river began to shell the camp. They had run up four globe—sighting 16 shotguns to the top of a small hill. We were too far from our guns and there were no orders given to shoot, so they shelled us a plenty.[51]

While the boys were watching the kettle a cannon ball struck the fire, upset the kettle, passed between the legs of one of the men and exploded a little farther on. This did not seem to cause any alarm. They had heard cannon balls explode before, but a mighty wail went up over the loss of the apple dumplings. The air was blue around there, and at that particular moment the boys would have charged the enemy joyously.

I was with the doctors that day. They had a negro who was a fine forager. He even brought us fried chicken. We had a royal spread in front of the doctors' tent and were consuming the good things with great relish, when a cannon ball went through the tent! It looked like it was going to smash us to smithereens, grub and all! We got away from there. We grabbed the grub and went down the line where we finished our meal. Not royally as we would have done, but hastily and stealthily.

But our sharpshooters in the dumps on the river

52. The withdrawal to Lafayette, Georgia, about twenty-two miles south of Chattanooga, was caused by Bragg's fear of being outflanked by Rosecrans. Most of Cleburne's brigades evacuated their positions along the river on September 6 and marched via Tyner's Gap to Chattanooga. On September 7, believing he could not hold Chattanooga, Bragg ordered the entire army, led by Cleburne's division, to push on to Lafayette. Most of Hill's corps arrived there on September 8. However, Bevens's recollection of leaving Gardenshire's Ferry and marching directly to Lafayette on September 10 may be correct, even though it would have been a long march—forty miles. General Hill reported on September 9 that two of Cleburne's regiments, "which had been picketing above Harrison had not yet joined him." The First Arkansas may have been one of these regiments. Purdue, *Pat Cleburne*, 207–09; OR, vol. 30, pt. 2, 138.

53. Bevens fails to explain the movements of Polk's brigade between September 10 and 19. Briefly, early on September 11, the brigade marched from Lafayette about five miles northward through Dug Gap in Pigeon Mountain to McLemore's Cove. Bragg had intended to use Cleburne's division in a coordinated attack against Union troops near there. Twice Cleburne's men began an advance, and twice they were halted. The division remained in position to guard against penetration of the gaps by Maj. Gen. George Henry Thomas's corps. On September 12, Polk's brigade advanced toward Rock Spring Church, about twelve miles north of Lafayette on the road to Lee and Gordon's Mills, to block another threatened Union advance. Again, no action occurred. The brigade apparently returned to Pigeon Mountain on September 13, but then the entire division passed through the region again on September 18, as Hill's corps took up a position along Chickamauga Creek, a few miles east of Lee and Gordon's Mills. The corps formed the left flank of the right wing of Bragg's army. Thomas L. Connelly, *Autumn of Glory: The Army of Tennessee, 1862–1865* (Baton Rouge: Louisiana State University Press, 1971), 174–89; Purdue, *Pat Cleburne,* 216; OR, vol. 30, pt. 2, 138–40.

got even with them. The Yanks drove out into the field with two six-mule wagons to get some fine rebel fodder. There were about thirty men in all, teamsters and guards. Some of them stood on the rail pen surrounding the fodder, others climbed on the shock to begin at the top. Our sharpshooters shot the mules first, then the men, and few lived to tell the tale. Sherman said, "War is Hell." In this case it was hell to them.

September 10th we marched down the valley toward Lafayette. As the dust was a foot deep and water scarce we moved slowly and we went into camp about ten o'clock.[52]

Dr. Scott of our Division, was sent for to see a citizen who was very ill. He went and relieved him, and left medicine, not asking pay for his services. After he had returned to camp a negro brought him a huge tray heaped with good things to eat. The doctor looked at the pile of grub, and said, "You boys must dine with me today, I can't eat all of this." We needed no further urging for our blue beef and water corn-dodger was rather poor fare. We lit into it, and as hungry wolves devour a sheep, so we devoured that pile of grub. Then the darkey took his tray and departed with a note of thanks. Our gratitude was truly sincere.

September 19th battle was on hand.[53] We were in

54. It would have been impossible to transfer Hardee's corps to Polk's brigade because a corps is larger than a brigade. It is possible that Bevens meant to say the brigade had been transferred to the corps, now commanded by General Hill, but that had occurred in July.

55. Lt. Gen. James Longstreet was detached from the Army of Northern Virginia on September 9 with the divisions of Maj. Gen. John Bell Hood and Maj. Gen. Lafayette McLaws, and Jenkins' Battery of Maj. Gen. George Edward Pickett's division, about six thousand men in all. His advance elements arrived at Chickamauga on September 19.

General Polk's Brigade, to which the Hardee Corps had been transferred.[54] When orders were read we found ourselves named as reserves. Cannonading began on our right, and we were moved quickly to the sound of the shot, about three miles. As we drew nearer to it we were ordered to double-quick. When we came to Chickamauga Creek we began to pull off our shoes to wade when General Cleburne came along saying, "Boys, go through that river, we can't wait."

Through the creek we went, and were among the first to be engaged instead of being reserves. When our line was deployed and ordered forward we were the very first. We struck stubborn western troops who knew how to fight. The conflict was terrific and raged all day. When night fell the engagement was stopped. Throwing out skirmishers we found that the lines were mixed up terribly. We were among the Yankees and they were calling, "What command is this?" It was midnight before the lines were reformed. Then we had a night's sleep on the ground, knowing that on the morrow some of us would fall in defense of our country—some of us would never see home and mother again. General Longstreet arrived in the night with re-inforcements, bringing a division from Virginia.[55] At daybreak the struggle was renewed. On both sides was the determination. "God being our helper, we will win this day." Wave after wave of

56. Such a sketchy description of the First Arkansas's dramatic role in the Battle of Chickamauga (September 19–20) is puzzling. For a better firsthand account see James L. Nichols and Frank Abbott, eds., "Reminiscences of Confederate Service by Wiley A. Washburn," *Arkansas Historical Quarterly,* 35 (Spring 1976), 57–59. Polk's brigade formed the right of Cleburne's division. It moved smartly forward in fighting on September 19 until darkness required a halt. Fighting on the second day was more rugged, and after a brief resumption of the previous day's advance, the brigade was repulsed with heavy losses. General Cleburne ordered Polk's men to fall back three hundred to four hundred yards to reform. When the Confederate attack was resumed in mid-afternoon, Polk's brigade "soon carried the northwestern angle of the enemy's works, taking in succession three lines of breastworks." OR, vol. 30, pt. 2, 153–58.

57. Casualties were actually about 34,624 (Federals 16,170; Confederates 18,454) of 124,548 engaged (Federals 58,222; Confederates 66,326). The First Arkansas lost 13 dead, 180 wounded, 1 missing. Company G had 2 dead and 10 wounded.

58. Longstreet's statement lends an element of interest to the comparison of the Army of Northern Virginia and the Army of Tennessee offered by Richard M. McMurry, *Two Great Rebel Armies: An Essay in Confederate Military History* (Chapel Hill: University of North Carolina Press, 1989).

59. Forrest is Brig. Gen. Nathan Bedford Forrest (1821–77), who commanded the Confederate cavalry corps at Chickamauga. Bevens was unaware of Forrest's orders and the predicament of his men and horses on September 20: "My command was kept on the field during the night of the 20th, and men and horses suffered greatly for want of water. The men were without rations, and the horses had only received a partial feed once during the two days' engagement." OR, vol. 30, pt. 2, 525.

deadly lead was sent against those Western troops, who contested every inch of the ground, who would stand a charge, and stay on the field. But our blood was hot, we fought for home, and against an invading foe and we could not give up at all. At the end of two days a battle of battles had been fought and won for the Confederate cause.[56] But alas, how many Southern boys had bitten the dust. The field was so thickly strewn with dead we could scarcely walk over it without stepping on the corpses. Our Regiment lost 42 killed and 103 wounded, and of the 120,000 men engaged on both sides, 28,000 were killed and wounded.[57]

Longstreet's men said to us, "Boys, you have tougher men to fight than we."[58]

If we had followed up our victory and had Forrest cut off the enemy's supplies what a difference it would have made. We might have stretched our lines to the Kentucky border. Such are the mistakes of war.[59]

At this battle one of the boys captured two horses and gave them to Dr. Arnold. He said he would draw feed for them and on the march I could ride one of them. I named my horse "General Thomas" but before we left our first camp the assistant surgeons could draw feed only for one horse so I was afoot as I had been for two years.

We established a line of breastworks on Missionary

60. As Rosecrans' army retreated toward Chattanooga, a town of just 5,500 at the start of the war, Bragg's army pursued. Cleburne's division advanced on September 21 to Red House Ford, across Chickamauga Creek, about five miles east of Rossville, Georgia. On September 22, the division moved onto the crest and eastern slope of Missionary Ridge, as Bragg laid siege to the Union army in Chattanooga. In late October, the division moved a mile southward along the ridge, so that its final position was again on the left flank of the army's right wing. Purdue, *Pat Cleburne*, 237–38. On September 30, Company G received another requisition of much-needed clothing. The most important item was a collection of 35 pairs of shoes, but the men also welcomed 17 pairs of drawers, 16 shirts, 10 jackets, and 8 pairs of pants. Requisition order in Captain Shoup's file, Service Records, Roll 51.

Another reorganization of the army took place while the First Arkansas was entrenched on Missionary Ridge. Most of the changes, inspired in part by a personal inspection of the army by Jefferson Davis in mid-October, were designed to eliminate officers who were critical of General Bragg. Changes affecting the First Arkansas included the return of General Hardee, whom President Davis regarded as a peacemaker, as corps commander and the consolidation of the Thirty-fifth and Forty-eighth Tennessee within the brigade. OR, vol. 31, pt. 3, 617; Woodworth, *Jefferson Davis and his Generals*, 238–44.

61. If Hottentots is meant to suggest black troops, Bevens is in error. There were no black troops at Chattanooga. Bevens seems to be confused about the name of the valley he describes. He is probably referring to the Chattanooga Valley, the plain between Chattanooga and Missionary Ridge. Wauhatchie is a town on the Nashville and Chattanooga Railroad south of the Tennessee River and west of Lookout Mountain. In the advance against Lookout Mountain, described by Bevens below, Maj. Gen. Joseph Hooker led his men from Bridgeport into the valley between Wauhatchie and Lookout Mountain (known as Lookout Valley) in late October. This prohibited Confederate forces from interfering with the Union "cracker line" that brought supplies into Chattanooga from the west. The Sequatchie Valley, west of Chattanooga, served as a funnel for some reinforcements and supplies headed for the Army of the Cumberland, but this valley could hardly be said to be swarming. See Ulysses S. Grant, "Chattanooga," in Robert Underwood Johnson and Clarence Clough Buel, eds., *Battles and Leaders of the Civil War,* 4 vols. (New York: Century Company, 1887), III, 687–91.

62. Thomas Carmichael Hindman (1828–68), a native of Tennessee and Mexican War veteran, moved to Arkansas in the 1850s and won election to Congress in 1858 and 1860. He entered the war as colonel of the Second Arkansas Infantry, but by September 1863 he was a major

Ridge and held Lookout Mountain, a mountain over a mile in height, and, as we thought, commanded Chattanooga.[60]

The Yankees saw that something must be done or things would be booming in Dixie. They brought to the front Dutch, Irish, Hottentots and all kinds of troops, and by the last of October the Sequatchie (Wauhatchie?) Valley was swarming like a beehive.[61]

Once a Dutch corp of 15,000 went down the valley through a gap to reach our rear. Bragg sent to meet them about 15,000 troops, placing them arrowed in front. He had a line under General Hindman with orders, at a certain signal, to rush across, cutting them off entirely from the main army. The signal was never given and we do not know why to this day. At that signal we were to follow across the valley at double-quick but Mr. Dutch discovered he was in a trap and he marched out again.[62]

There was a Union man living on the route of this Dutch Devil, who had not joined either army. He had lived on his farm unmolested by the Southern troops, and supposed that of course he would be protected by the Northern troops. As the Dutch marched down to attack us they stopped at this man's home, searched the place, insulted his wife and knocked him down. As they came running back they had no time to tarry, but one at a time, a straggler would drop into his smokehouse to see if there was general and divisional commander in the Army of Tennessee. However, the incident described by Bevens goes unrecorded in the official records, and there is no evidence of Hindman participating in any such maneuvers. In fact, Hindman was in General Bragg's doghouse at this time for having disobeyed orders prior to Chickamauga. He was relieved of his command on September 29. Woodworth, *Jefferson Davis and His Generals*, 239.

W. T. Barnes

63. As with several of Bevens's stories, this one about the Union man cannot be verified, although incidents such as this one certainly did occur.

64. The battle of Lookout Mountain, not the entire three days of fighting at Chattanooga, is often referred to as the "Battle Above the Clouds" because of the fog and mist that obscured the 1,100-foot peak when Union troops under General Hooker attacked it on the morning of November 24. The First Arkansas, perched along Missionary Ridge, did not participate in this battle.

The First Arkansas nearly missed the battle of Missionary Ridge, too, as Cleburne's division had been evacuated on November 23 to Chickamauga Station. The division was to be transported to Knoxville via the Western and Atlantic Railroad in order to join in the siege against that town when it was suddenly recalled and thrown into a position on the northern end of Missionary Ridge, on Tunnel Hill. Cleburne positioned Polk's brigade and Semple's battery at the northeastern base of Missionary Ridge, below Tunnel Hill, to defend the East Tennessee and Georgia Railroad bridge over Chickamauga Creek. The First Arkansas, which engaged only in what General Cleburne called "heavy skirmishing," held its position, but as units around it began to crumble, the First Arkansas fell in with the general Confederate withdrawal. The regiment suffered no casualties in the fighting, although the division lost 250 men. Hughes, *General William J. Hardee,* 169–76; OR, vol. 31, pt. 2, 745–46, 752.

one ham left. The Union man took a long, keen bowie-knife and stood in the dark corner of the smokehouse; when only one man entered he stabbed him to the heart and put his body into the well. He killed three men. Next morning, he with his wife and children, walked into our camp. He said he was ready to fight to the bitter end. He took his family South and came back and made a bad soldier for them.[63]

November 23, 24 and 25 we fought the "Battle Above the Clouds," the terrible conflict of Lookout Mountain and Missionary Ridge. We were fighting continuously during those three days. We were in breastworks on the ridge near Lookout Mountain, but when the fighting was fiercest we were sent to relieve the commands at the extreme right of the Yankee army. They came in solid front five columns deep and charged our breastworks but were driven back hour after hour with terrible slaughter. Late in the afternoon they made a concentrated attack on our center and drove our men out of line. We had to give up Lookout Mountain and we retreated to the Ridge about midnight. Throughout the night Sherman's troops were coming up, and next day we were attacked in front and flank. Our breastworks were of no use as Lookout Mountain commanded the Ridge, so in spite of desperate struggles we were ordered to retreat.[64]

65. "Sheckle" (taken from the Hebrew word "shekel," a measurement of 1/2 ounce of gold or silver) is nineteenth-century slang for money. Thus "sheckle luck" is gambling.

66. Casper K. Burnett, from Washington County, Kentucky, enlisted in Company G at Knoxville in September 1862. He stood 5'7" and had blue eyes, light hair, and a fair complexion. Service Records, Roll 46.

67. Bevens does not mean to say the entire regiment reached Dalton, Georgia, that same night. The army arrived at Dalton, about thirty miles southeast of Chattanooga, on November 28. Cleburne's division served as rear guard for the army during the three-day withdrawal and forded the South Chickamauga Creek early on the morning of November 27. Purdue, *Pat Cleburne,* 253–54.

At Chattanooga it had been agreed that there should be no firing on the line of pickets without notification. Here between the picket line and the main line of battle our sporting boys sought "sheckle luck," those who were fortunate enough to have a few sheckles of Confederate money.[65] One day when General Hardee was officer of the day he ordered a regiment deployed around the gamblers, but soldiers from all parts of the field yelled to the boys to run, and run they did. General Hardee did not get many.

In our company was a Kentucky lad named Burnett who had a brother in the Union Army. They got permission to spend the day together. When the day was over they separated, each going back to his command. That was a war! Brother against brother, father against son, arrayed in deadly combat.[66]

We went to Dalton, marching all night. As we crossed the river it seemed the coldest night our thinly clad men had ever experienced. Our corp under Hardee was the rear guard. General Cleburne's Division was immediately in the rear. General Polk was our Brigadier General. About two o'clock we passed General Cleburne mounted, looking and thinking.[67]

"Something is going to happen" I said to the boys. "Why?"

"Look at General Cleburne, don't you see war in his eyes?"

68. John M. W. Baird was promoted to corporal in 1862 but then reduced to private in August 1863. According to the census of 1860, he was fifteen when the war started and lived with a sister, Jane Baird (age twenty-three), in the boardinghouse of Julia Wood. Both John and Jane had been born in Arkansas. Service Records, Roll 46.

69. The action described here is a continuation of the rear guard defense en route to Dalton. Having forded South Chickamauga Creek, the division was frantically ordered to turn and buy time for the Confederate baggage and artillery trains to pass through Ringgold Gap, about twelve miles northwest of Dalton between White Oak Mountain and Taylor's Ridge. Cleburne, early on the morning of November 27, directed the First Arkansas "to take [a] position temporarily near the rear mouth of the gap with directions to observe my right flank and prevent the enemy from turning me in that quarter." General Polk then learned from a Confederate straggler that Federal troops were preparing to outflank Cleburne by crossing White Oak Mountain on the right. Polk ordered the First Arkansas up the gently rising slope of the mountain, where the regiment "found the skirmishers of the enemy within 20 steps of the top." A see-saw battle ensued, but the Federals were finally pushed back. Some men did, indeed, resort to hurling rocks down on the Federals. The First Arkansas captured twenty prisoners and the battle flag of the Seventy-sixth Ohio Infantry. Cleburne praised the First Arkansas for "its courage and constancy." Connelly, *Autumn of Glory,* 276–77; Hammock, *With Honor Untarnished,* 105–107; OR, vol. 31, pt. 2, 755–56, 760–61. For maps tracing the complicated movement from Missionary Ridge to Ringgold Gap see Purdue, *Pat Cleburne,* between pages 320 and 321.

The colors of the Seventy-sixth Ohio had been captured by John Cathey, John Loftin, Billy Barnes, and Lon Steadman, of Company G, after eight Ohio color bearers had been shot. In 1916, in a grand ceremony at Newark, Ohio, several surviving members of the First Arkansas, including Cathey, Steadman, and Bevens, returned the flag to survivors of the Seventy-sixth Ohio. See *Confederate Veteran* 25 (March 1917), 131, 136 (April 1917), 185; 28 (February 1920), 71; William E. Bevens Memorandum Book, courtesy of Lady Elizabeth Watson.

We had crossed Ringgold Mountain, but we were sent back to take the horses from the cannon, put men in their places, and pulled it quickly to the top of the mountain, so to the summit over rocks and between trees two pieces were carried. Our regiment was sent to the top with them. Two minutes more would have been too late. Not fifty yards away on the other side of the hill were Yankees climbing for the same goal. Then the firing began. We had the advantage in having a tree to use as breastworks, and in being able to see them. Whenever one stepped aside from his tree to shoot our men got him. Captain Shoup and John Baird rolled rocks down the hill and when a Yankee dodged the other boys shot him.[68] We picked off dozens. When the cannon was got ready and began shelling the woods, breaking the trees, tearing up rocks and showering them on the lines below, they had to break and retreat in haste down the hill.

If we had not got there as soon as we did our line would have been the one to retreat.[69]

General Cleburne took us next to Ringgold Gap, a gap dug by the railroad through the mountain. He made a talk to the boys, telling us that we were there to save the army, which was five miles away and could not possibly get help to us. Our task would require nerve and will of which he knew we had plenty. We were to form two lines of battle across the

70. After the action on Taylor's Ridge and White Oak Mountain, Cleburne withdrew a mile beyond Ringgold Gap and prepared for another assault. Cleburne fired into the advancing Union ranks, but the Federals declined to attack. The Union casualties mentioned by Bevens must have resulted from the artillery fire. The Confederate casualties he gives are for the division; the First Arkansas suffered few losses. Hammock, *With Honor Untarnished*, 108–09; OR, vol. 31, pt. 2, 757.

gap and were not to fire until he gave the signal, (by signs, as commands would not be heard in the roar of guns.)

The Yankees having failed to break our line on the mountain had massed their forces at the gap, determined to break Cleburne's line, when the rest would be easy for them.

They came on seven columns deep to our two. We watched them advance and seconds seemed hours. We felt they would be on us before Cleburne ever gave the signal. Would he never give it? At last when the time was ripe, he, who knew the art of war so well, gave the signal to fire, and such deadly work did we perform as was not surpassed in the whole four years of war. We let loose on them four pieces of cannon. The command to stop firing was not given until the number of dead in our front was greater than our Brigade. This fight showed strategy and bravery. It checked the advance of an army five times greater than our Division, and it proved to General Hardee that he had one man who could plan and execute a battle with any adversary. Ever after, Cleburne with his Arkansas, Tennessee and Texas men was placed in the hottest part of battle. Our loss was 88 killed, 23 wounded, and their loss was reported in Northern papers as 2,000 killed, wounded and captured.[70]

71. Cleburne's division fell back three miles from Ringgold Gap on the night of November 27 toward Dalton. He halted at Tunnel Hill, Georgia, about ten miles northwest of Dalton, where the First Arkansas received its first rations in two days and settled into winter camp. During the next few months, Company G received five requisitions of clothing, issued between November 30, 1863, and March 31, 1864. These included seventy-nine pairs of pants, fifty-nine pairs of drawers, forty-two pairs of shoes, forty-two shirts, twenty-nine jackets, twenty-seven hats, and twenty-one pairs of socks, plus assorted pots, pans, and tools. Requisition orders in Captain Shoup's file, Service Records, Roll 51.

72. Shin-plasters were paper money of small denominations issued by private banks and businesses.

73. Atlanta had the Confederacy's largest pharmaceutical laboratory until, before the fall of the city in 1864, it was moved to Augusta. By November 1863, Atlanta had been swamped with hundreds of wounded soldiers from the fighting at Chickamauga and Chattanooga. Drugs would have been in great demand, so it is no wonder that Bevens had to go on to Augusta. Cunningham, *Doctors in Gray,* 146–47. For an insightful discussion of pharmaceuticals in the Confederacy see Norman H. Franke, *Pharmaceutical Conditions and Drug Supply in the Confederacy* (Madison, Wis.: American Institute of the History of Pharmacy, 1955). For a firsthand account of the hospitals in and around Atlanta in the autumn of 1863 see Richard Barksdale Harwell, ed., *Kate: The Journal of a Confederate Nurse* (Baton Rouge: Louisiana State University Press, 1959), 144–84.

We went into winter quarters at Dalton, our regiment being in front of the general army. We camped near Tunnel Hill.[71] We had good foraging ground and could get chickens, eggs, butter, so we lived high. John Loftin was captain of the foragers and he was a good one too. He only got caught once but he lied out of that. Two negroes, who belonged to two doctors of our Brigade, went to Dalton one night to see the sights and buy half-moon pies, big sorghum ginger-bread, and other things. Coming home at midnight they were crossing a railroad trestle when two robbers called on them to halt. Sam began to parley with them when whack! they hit him over the head, and told him to give up his money. He yielded up his shin-plasters, all he had.[72] They then took Tom's can. He did not have much so they told him to pull. He was a good runner especially when scared, and he lit out over rocks and brush, beating his partner to camp. With eyes as big as saucers he related his exploits to his master. They did not visit Dalton at night again. We used to go over there to see the girls and have parties and sorghum "candy pulls." It was a great diversion, and between the lines, when the guards were on to it they would arrest, but the boys could usually outgeneral them.

From this camp I was sent on a three days' furlough to Augusta to buy some drug supplies not to be found in Atlanta.[73] When I reached Atlanta whom

74. Brig. Gen. John Hunt Morgan (1825–64) was captured in July 1863 near Lisbon, Ohio. He escaped from a Federal prison in November and accepted a new command in Southwest Virginia. He traveled to Atlanta to inspect his rebuilt unit in February 1864, at which time he was feted and honored by the city. Garrett, *Atlanta,* I, 563–64.

75. According to the census of 1860, George Washington Roberts was born about 1836 and worked as a blacksmith in Independence County. He, his wife Martha, and their eldest child had been born in Tennessee. Two younger children had been born in Missouri before the family settled in Arkansas about 1859. Roberts spent most of the war working as quartermaster, and from July 1863 through August 1864 he was detached to General Morgan's command. Service Records, Roll 51.

76. Peter Snyder commanded the Sixth and Seventh Arkansas (Consolidated) in the brigade of Brig. Gen. St. John Richardson Liddell, of Cleburne's division. He, too, had fought at Chickamauga, Missionary Ridge, and Ringgold Gap. He apparently died in North Carolina in 1864. OR, vol. 30, pt. 2, pp. 14, 266–67, vol. 31, pt. 2, pp. 766–67, pt. 3, p. 617, vol. 45, pt. 1, p. 667; *Confederate Veteran* 16 (July 1908), 348.

77. According to the census of 1860, Edward M. Dickinson was born about 1840 in Batesville, Independence County, where he worked as a bookkeeper. His father, born in New York, was a farmer and businessman who, for a few years, owned a hotel in Batesville. Dickinson returned to Batesville after the war. He served as county clerk 1874–86, and he frequently conducted services as a lay preacher at the Episcopal church in the mid-1880s. James Logan Morgan, trans., *Independence County, Arkansas, Seventh Census Free Population Schedules 1850* (Newport, Ark.: Northeast Arkansas Genealogical Association, 1971), 61; *Biographical and Historical Memoirs of Northeast Arkansas* (Chicago: Goodspeed Publishing Company, 1889), 622, 661; John Q. Wolf, "My Fifty Years in Batesville, Arkansas," eds. Nancy Britton and Nana Farris, *Independence County Chronicle* 23 (October 1981–January 1982), 10.

The census of 1860 shows that Benjamin Adler was born in Germany about 1834. He was living with A. Adler, a thirty-year-old Jackson County merchant worth twenty-six thousand dollars, when the war started.

Charles A. Bridewell enlisted as a private in the Sixth Arkansas Infantry when the war started. He was promoted to lieutenant in that regiment before being transferred to the Seventh Arkansas, where he served as quartermaster and captain. Desmond Walls Allen, comp., *Index to Arkansas Confederate Soldiers,* 3 vols. (Conway, Ark.: D. W. Allen, 1990), I, 61. I have been unable to identify Major Moon.

should I meet but George Roberts, one of my old mess-mates who had been transferred to Morgan's Cavalry. Morgan had been captured, and all that was left of the command was at Macon re-organizing.[74] George was buying horses. He was flush and wanted me to take a thousand dollars, but I had lots of money, at least for these days. He went to the depot to see me off. Roberts was a fine fellow. He was a regular city rat. We country boys used to get him to pilot us around the city. He would know all the streets in a day and could take us anywhere we wanted to go. After the war he settled in Texas, where he was cashier of a bank. He died several years ago.[75]

In Augusta I met Colonel Snyder of the Eighth Arkansas. He was from Pocahontas, Ark., and was then on a furlough.[76] I also met Ed M. Dickinson, Thad Kinman and Ben Adler. They belonged to the quartermaster's department under Captain Bridewell and Major Moon.[77] They kept books as big as a dining table. As they belonged to this particular department they helped me to draw a new jacket suit. They lived in a fine city and fared sumptuously, so knowing all the ropes they made it mighty pleasant for me. Through Ed I met an uncle whom I had not seen before. It was on a crowded street in the city, but I knew him at once from his resemblance to my father.

78. Bevens's uncle was Thomas H. Bevens, who lived in the third ward of Augusta. According to the census of 1860, he worked as a dentist and had a family of five. His wife, Angeline, was forty-five years old (two years his junior), and their four children ranged in age from seven to thirteen. The youngest child was a boy named William.

79. Bevens fails to indicate whether he secured any drugs in Augusta, although, as in Atlanta, they would have been in high demand. Still, Augusta, with a population of 12,500 (8,500 white) in 1860, had been little touched by the war. In September 1863, one visitor declared Augusta to be a "pleasant little city." He went on to report, "To judge from Augusta, no one would have supposed that two formidable armies were confronting each other within a twenty-four hours' journey. Every one seemed engrossed in business, and shops were all plenteously filled with stores and customers." Augusta was deemed so safe by Confederate authorities that it had become one of the South's principal gunpowder and armaments manufacturing centers. However, the situation began to change by November 1863. The city was suddenly flooded with wounded soldiers. Prices for all goods shot up, a result, in part, of the large number of refugees seeking havens in the city. By December 1863, butter cost $3.50 per pound, eggs $2 per dozen, coffee $10 per pound, pork $1.25 per pound, women's shoes $30 per pair, and firewood $23 per cord. If Bevens's friends were living well it was because of their military rank and association with the quartermaster department. Fitzgerald Ross, *Cities and Camps of the Confederate States,* ed. Richard Barksdale Harwell (Urbana: University of Illinois Press, 1958), 115, 141–42; Florence Fleming Corley, *Confederate City: Augusta, Georgia, 1860–1865* (Columbia: University of South Carolina Press, 1960), 68–72, 78; *Augusta Chronicle and Sentinel,* 2 December 1863, 3.

80. Johnston is Gen. Joseph Eggleston Johnston (1807–91), a West Point graduate and Mexican War veteran who had won his early laurels fighting in Virginia. He replaced Bragg as commander of the Army of Tennessee in December 1863. In January 1864, a tremor, of which Bevens was probably unaware, ran through the high command of the army when General Cleburne drafted a long, impassioned manifesto to General Johnston imploring the use of black troops in the Confederate army. Cleburne, appalled by the thinness of his ranks (some companies could muster no more than a few dozen men), believed that southern independence could be secured only by sacrificing the institution of slavery. "Slavery," he wrote, "from being one of our chief strengths at the commencement of the war, has now become, in a military point of view, one of our chief sources of weakness." The letter was cosigned by most of Cleburne's brigade and regimental commanders, including Colonel Colquitt and Colonel Snyder. Purdue,

When I accosted him he was very dignified and seemed to doubt me until I told him the names of the whole family. Then he insisted upon me going to his home. He had an interesting family. My grandmother died at his home and was buried in a cemetery in Augusta.[78] I got back to camp on time. After living off the fat of the land our regular diet of blue beef and corn bread somehow failed to tickle the palate. George Thomas, who had been wounded at Murfreesboro, got back to us at this camp.[79]

We were waiting to move on the checkerboard. Jeff Davis, General Bragg, Johnston and all were calling for the troops to have a decisive battle hereabouts, but there was a difference of opinion between Davis and the commanding generals.[80] Our Brigade was ordered, I suppose, to Mississippi. We went by rail to Montgomery, were halted there, and were sent back to Dalton and went into camp again.[81]

May 8th, 1864 we began the famous Dalton campaign, under the leadership of the superb General Joseph E. Johnston. He had between forty and fifty thousand men divided into three corps, commanded respectively by Generals Hardee, Hood and Polk. He was opposed by Sherman with about 100,000 well drilled seasoned soldiers by Generals Thomas, McPherson and Schofield, but Johnston was equal to the campaign.[82]

Pat Cleburne, 267–78; OR, vol. 52, pt. 2, 586–92. See also Robert F. Durden, *The Gray and the Black: The Confederate Debate on Emancipation* (Baton Rouge: Louisiana State University, 1972).

81. Hardee's entire corps moved toward Alabama in late February to block a potential threat from Maj. Gen. William Tecumseh Sherman in Mississippi, but the plan was aborted and the corps was ordered back to Georgia. Cleburne's division arrived at Atlanta on February 24–25, then moved to a new camp at Mill Creek, three miles east of Dalton. While at Mill Creek, a member of the First Arkansas was shot for persistent desertion. This was the only military execution ever to take place in Cleburne's division. Purdue, *Pat Cleburne,* 291–93; Hammock, *With Honor Untarnished,* 111–12; Watkins, *Co. Aytch,* 130–31.

Surprisingly, Bevens fails to mention the great snowball fight that took place between the brigades of General Polk and Brig. Gen. Daniel Chevilette Govan (formerly colonel of the Second Arkansas Infantry) following a four-inch snowfall in late March. Ben LaBree, ed., *Camp Fires of the Confederacy* (Louisville: Courier-Journal Printing Company, 1898), 48–53. The Dalton camp also experienced the enthusiasm of a religious revival that swept through many Confederate camps during the winter of 1863–64. Bevens, being an Episcopalian, more than likely did not engage in this largely Methodist-Baptist-Presbyterian movement. Nichols and Abbott, eds.,

"Reminiscences of Confederate Service," 62; *Confederate Veteran* 28 (April 1920), 130–32; Drew Gilpen Faust, "Christian Soldiers: The Meaning of Revivalism in the Confederate Army," *Journal of Southern History* 53 (February 1987), 62–63, 72–83.

82. Bevens here describes the onset of the Atlanta campaign, in which Johnston, faced with three advancing Federal armies under Sherman, conducted a six-week Fabian withdrawal. Union forces, totaling 98,500 men, included the Army of the Cumberland (commanded by General Thomas), Army of the Tennessee (commanded by Maj. Gen. James Birdseye McPherson), and Army of the Ohio (commanded by Maj. Gen. John McAllister Schofield). Johnston had 45,000 men at Dalton, although another 18,000 would soon join him from Mississippi. Polk's brigade entered the campaign having been significantly reorganized in late April. The First Arkansas had been so depleted that it was consolidated with the Fifteenth Arkansas; the consolidated regiment was commanded by Lt. Col. William H. Martin. Martin had begun the war as captain of the Ettomon Guards, Pulaski County, which became Company F in the First Arkansas. He had only recently returned to duty after having been severely wounded at Ringgold Gap. The brigade's other regiments included the Fifth Confederate, Second Tennessee, Thirty-fifth Tennessee, and Forty-eighth Tennessee. Hammock, *With Honor Untarnished,* 9, 109; OR, vol. 32, pt. 3, 867.

This was the Federal view of Cheatham's thrust up the Columbia
Pike toward Franklin. Federals held the stone wall in foreground.
*(Courtesy Massachusetts Commandery Military Order of the Loyal
Legion and the U.S. Army Military History Institute.)*

83. The opening engagement of the campaign was at Rocky Face Ridge (May 5–11). Cleburne moved two brigades from Mill Creek to Dug Gap, a pass in Rocky Face Ridge about five miles southwest of Dalton, on May 8. Polk's brigade was not one of them, although it apparently did shift its position. When the rest of the division moved forward on May 10, Polk's brigade marched to within a mile of Resaca before turning, after a two- to three-hour halt, and marching back to Dug Gap, which it reached about sundown. Thus the brigade marched thirty-three miles as Bevens mentions. Cleburne reported, "My division was now altogether." The march to Snake Creek Gap began at 7 A.M. on May 11. After halting for several hours, Cleburne resumed the march and halted at sundown about ten miles south of Dalton. Here, along Sugar Creek Road, the men threw up breastworks on May 12 in anticipation of a Federal attack. The attack did not come, so on May 13, the division moved to a ridge west of Resaca. OR, vol. 38, pt. 3, 720–21. For a broader picture of these movements see Connelly, *Autumn of Glory*, 336–43.

84. The battle of Resaca (May 13–16) consisted mostly of skirmishing, but Johnston was forced to fall back to a line north and west of Resaca when his position on Rocky Face Ridge was turned from the west by McPherson's army. Cleburne withdrew his division at about 10 P.M. on May 15 to cross the Oostanaula River by means of a trestle bridge. OR, vol. 38, pt. 3, 722.

May 8th we were menaced by the enemy in front and flank. May 9th we moved our position two miles to the left and on May 10th we moved rapidly back to the top of the mountain. We had no tents nor protection of any kind. We slept on the ground among the rocks. Although it rained in torrents, we were so dead tired from our 33 mile march, we did not know it was raining until we were wet through. At daybreak we were again on the march and went to Snake Creek Gap, then three miles to the left and built breastworks. From there we marched to Resaca.[83] May 15th we had heavy fighting and were forced from our position. The retreat was covered by Hardee's corps. Our engineers had to build, under fire, a bridge for the army to cross the Oostanaula.[84] In fact from Dalton to Atlanta we had a continuous battle. We moved back slowly, and only when flanked and outnumbered. When we adopted a new line a few miles back, we built breastworks. Thus marching, battling, building works, in rain and mud, with no camp, no tents and but little food, the campaign went on. But in all our skirmishes and engagements we used every advantage to their great loss. We fell back to Calhoun, then to Adairsville. We were the rear guard on that road. After we had crossed a creek and marched to the top of the hill, (our Cavalry to the rear), the Yankees moved opposite and opened

85. Having crossed the Oostanaula, Cleburne halted at midnight near Calhoun, Georgia, about five miles south of Resaca. Polk's brigade became "briskly engaged with the enemy's skirmishers" on May 16 near Calhoun. At 1 A.M. the next morning, Cleburne continued his withdrawal toward Adairsville, nearly ten miles south of Calhoun, and arrived about two miles north of the town at daylight. OR, vol. 38, pt. 3, 722–23.

86. General Jackson is probably Brig. Gen. John King Jackson (1828–66), who commanded a brigade in Maj. Gen. William Henry Talbot Walker's division.

87. With the Federals in hot pursuit, Cleburne moved further south toward Cassville in the early morning of May 18. He arrived about two miles north of the town at 4 P.M. Polk's brigade, still serving as rear guard, finally joined the division on May 19. OR, vol 38, pt. 3, 723. For the broader picture see Connelly, *Autumn of Glory,* 343–47.

up a battery. We were ordered to lie down and not to fire until told to do so.[85] General Polk and General Jackson rode in front of us and the sharpshooters and artillery of the enemy made it hot for them, bullets going through their hats and clothes.[86] General Jackson would dodge, but General Polk would sit as straight as an arrow and never move a muscle. I heard him when he told General Cleburne and asked permission to advance on the enemy. When the courier returned General Cleburne himself came to see the fun. From our hill could be seen fifty thousand Yankee troops—Infantry, Cavalry and Artillery. For our Brigade to advance against such a force was a visionary idea, and the permission was not given.

We moved on to join our main army which was a few miles in front drawn up in line of battle near Cassville.[87] Our line was in open field, five miles long. Each man had forty cartridges and knew how to use them. General Johnston rode along the line and told the men he was going to give battle. The soldiers threw their caps into the air and shouted themselves hoarse with joy at the thought of going into a fight which they felt in their souls would be successful. It was inspiring to see such enthusiasm in battle scarred veterans who knew what fighting meant. It was not theory with them, it was knowledge gained in bloody experience. I was glad I was

88. Lyman B. Gill, who is not mentioned in the text, was born in New Jersey (one source says New York) in 1826. When the war started, Gill, who published and edited the *Jacksonport Herald* with Frank W. Lynn, left the paper to enlist as a private in the Jackson Guards. He rose to the rank of sergeant. Gill returned to Jacksonport after the war and married Jane A. Baird, the sister of John M. W. Baird, in 1867. Watson, *Fight and Survive!*, 2, 27; Service Records, Roll 47; Foster, *Marriage and Divorce Records*, 41.

Lyman B. Gill[88]

89. Generals Hood and Leonidas Polk opposed holding the Cassville line because, with Thomas closing in from the west and Schofield from the north, they feared the army would be vulnerable to enfilading fire. Withdrawal occurred on the night of May 19–20. For the controversy among the generals see Connelly, *Autumn of Glory*, 347–53, and Woodworth, *Jefferson Davis and his Generals*, 274–77.

on that field and saw that flashing of Southern bravery. Such patriots are born only of liberty-loving
people, born of God. That confidence of success, that
confidence in their leader was what Joseph E.
Johnston had looked for, had prayed for. He knew
his position to be the best he had ever had. He now
knew the temper of his men. Nothing could have
checked them. It would be the biggest battle of the
war and his success.

When this great battle was formed in Johnston's
brain and the Generals ordered to occupy the ground
assigned to them, who was the first to say he could
not hold his position? Who, but General Hood!
Histories love to state that these generals led their
men, but here was a time when the general did not
lead into battle the bravest men in the world who
were clamoring for the fight.

General Polk also expressed his disapproval of the
movement. When his two generals went back on
him, Johnston was paralyzed and could not or did
not attempt to carry out his plan. Unlike Albert
Sidney Johnston at Shiloh, who, when his plan was
disapproved of, and obstacles thrown in his way,
arose like the giant hero he was and said "You who
are true, go to your commands. The battle will begin
at daybreak." If he had lived a few hours longer he
would have won that battle beyond a doubt.[89]

90. Bevens errs by placing the First Arkansas in General Govan's brigade. Lucius Polk still commanded the Arkansans, although reorganization of the army and a severe wound to Polk would place them under Govan's command in June.

91. Current historical opinion on Johnston's strategy in Georgia is mixed but tends to be critical. See Herman Hattaway and Archer Jones, *How the North Won: A Military History of the Civil War* (Urbana: University of Illinois Press, 1983), 596–99, 604–07, and Woodworth, *Jefferson Davis and His Generals,* 277–85.

If Joseph E. Johnston had said something like this the men would have done the rest, but when he ordered the line under the skirmish fire to retreat they obeyed like true soldiers. It was a bitter disappointment, but their trust in the great commander was firm. He hoped that other opportunities would offer but when the time came he was relieved and the command given to that General who had thwarted the greatest battle of the Confederacy.

Johnston's plan of campaign was the only one possible for us, fighting against such odds. I am not a general, nor the son of a general, but having been right on the ground for four years, feel that I am entitled to an opinion. And so with all the men who composed Company G, First Arkansas Regiment, Hardee Corps, Govan Brigade, Cleburne Division. The verdict of these men who helped make history is that if Johnston's tactics had prevailed the Confederacy would have had a different tale to tell at Atlanta.[90]

Tacticians now agree that Johnston's success in preserving his army almost entire was an achievement of the greatest military science.[91]

May 19th we left Cassville. We marched mostly by night, built breastworks, and by daybreak were ready for the contest. On May 26th the heaviest assault on our works took place. On our skirmish line, a short

92. Between May 19 and 25, Cleburne's division fell steadily back with the rest of the army. He halted at Willford's Mill on Pumpkin Vine Creek, where Hardee's entire corps camped about three miles south of Etowah and two miles east of Alatoona on May 23. Then began a series of marches, countermarches, and bivouacs that finally brought Cleburne's men to the aid of General Hindman's division (General Hood's corps) at mid-afternoon on May 26, by which time Hindman's men had already been in action for the better part of a day. This was the battle of New Hope Church, a Methodist church located four miles northwest of Dallas, Georgia, fought May 25–27. Cleburne's men formed the extreme right of the Confederate line, anchored on New Hope Church. Dallas anchored the Confederate left. OR, vol. 38, pt. 3, 723–24; Connelly, *Autumn of Glory,* 354–55.

93. The brunt of the Federal attack at New Hope Church fell on Cleburne's men on May 27, near Pickett's Mill, nearly four miles northeast of New Hope Church. Their brilliant stand against a powerful assault saved the army's right wing and denied Sherman an opportunity to cut Johnston's communications with Atlanta. Purdue, *Pat Cleburne,* 322.

However, the First Arkansas did not actively participate in the Pickett's Mill fight. General Cleburne states quite clearly in his report: "During these operations Polk was not engaged, but it [his brigade] was a source of strength and confidence to the rest of the division to know that he had charge of the weakest and most delicate part of our line." OR, vol. 38, pt. 3, 726. Thus, Lt. Allie T. Walthall was not killed at Pickett's Mill but at Kenesaw Mountain, about a month later. Walthall, who worked as a clerk before the war, had enlisted as a private in Company G at age twenty. He was promoted to lieutenant in April 1862, just prior to the battle of Shiloh. His distant relative was Maj. Gen. Edward Cary Walthall (1831–98). Service Records, Roll 52.

distance in front of our works we had dump holes dug in the ground, the dirt thrown out facing the enemy. Thirty men stayed in the dumps until the main line came up. Then they opened fire and checked the advance. When they could no longer do this, they ran back to the line behind the breast-works.[92]

At New Hope Church the enemy made a seven line concentrated assault on our line. Our men were cool and steady, and all were splendid shots. We waited until they were very near, then sent forth a sheet of fire and lead that could not be withstood. The number of their dead was enormous, and our own loss was considerable. We lost our first lieu-tenant, Allie Walthall, here. He was a distant relative of General Walthall, and as brave a man as ever lived on earth.[93]

A lieutenant of another company was killed also. He was in one of the dumps with one of the sixteen rifles. He had seen four Yankees fall under his well-directed fire, but at last was mortally wounded. He backed out of the dump and into a hollow where the enemy could see him fall. His comrades went out and brought him behind the breastworks. As he lay on the ground he conversed with his friends urging them to become Christians. Sending for the Colonel, he told him that he (the colonel) was a wicked man,

94. I have been unable to identify this lieutenant, although it may have been either Andrew J. Pinter, of Company B, or Henry W. Norsworthy, of Company H, the only other two lieutenants (besides Walthall) who can be identified as having been killed during the Atlanta campaign. Hammock, *With Honor Untarnished*, 145, 155.

95. Johnston had shifted his line from New Hope Church on June 4 to a position on Lost, Pine, and Brush mountains. As Sherman's army pursued, skirmishing resumed on June 10. Cleburne's division was originally positioned on the northwestern edge of Kenesaw Mountain, near Gilgal Church, but it changed position twice during the next fortnight. The final position mentioned by Bevens was on a ridge of the western side of the mountain that bent back to the southwest of Marietta and ran to the Dallas Road. When the Federals moved into a position opposite Cleburne's line, each side found itself on a slight rise with a gully about one hundred yards wide separating them. Cleburne's line was spread thin (it looked "rather lonesome" as one veteran recalled). Breastworks were erected, and the First Arkansas added to its protective wall by cutting hundreds of saplings, sharpening their ends, and erecting them as abatis. "It would have been an uphill business for a rabbitt to creep through," wrote Billy Barnes. "At any rate, enough to cause the Yanks to *bide a wee*." Purdue, *Pat Cleburne*, 329–22; Gilbert E. Govan and James W. Livingood, *A Different*

Valor: The Story of General Joseph E. Johnston (Indianapolis: Bobbs-Merrill, 1956), 290–91; *Confederate Veteran* 30 (February 1922), 49.

As for the weather, one Arkansas soldier recalled, "The Rain Fell in Torrents and the Entire Country was so cut up with wagon and artilery that the mud and water was at least Knee Deep and in Places the Branches and Creeks was Waist Deep and it was so Dark that a man Could not see his file Leader half the Time." Worley, ed., *They Never Came Back*, 92.

96. Gen. Leonidas Polk was killed June 14 on Pine Mountain while reconnoitering Sherman's army. Two days later, his nephew, Gen. Lucius Polk, the First Arkansas's brigade commander, was wounded for the fourth time during the war and forced to retire from active service. His old brigade was broken up, and the First and Fifteenth Arkansas transferred to General Govan's brigade.

97. While Bevens was in Marietta, the rest of his regiment made a not uncommon arrangement with a Federal regiment, the Ninetieth Ohio Infantry, positioned "within a stone's throw" of the Confederate lines. The two regiments had clashed frequently ever since the fighting at Chattanooga. A survivor of the Ohio regiment recalled, "We became quite well acquainted with them [First Arkansas], and found them honorable, brave, and gallant soldiers." On Kenesaw Mountain, the two regiments agreed, explained the Ohioan, "not to fire at each other unless we came out of our works in line of battle. . . . This gave

and must lead a better life. By way of comfort one of the boys told him how many Yankees he had killed in the assault. The lieutenant said, "Yes, I killed three. But, my brother, don't gloat over it. Do your duty, but don't gloat over it." After sending many loving messages home he passed away.[94]

Meanwhile Sherman was receiving re-inforcements, and on June 9th moved against our intrenchments along Lost Mountains. In this region there was fighting for several days in the midst of almost incessant rain.[95] General Polk was killed during this engagement.[96] June 15–17 we abandoned both mountains and fell back to the great Kenesaw overlooking Marietta.

June 20th two of us got a permit to go to Marietta for tobacco and other supplies. As we were passing through the residence part of the city a kind-hearted lady invited us into the house to eat raspberries with her family. We did not have the heart to refuse her hospitality, so we went in. We had raspberries, cream and cake. Think of it, rebel soldiers regaled with such delicacies! When we got back to camp we told the boys about it and they said we lied! But the memory of that kind act to strangers and common privates will last as long as life itself.[97]

On the 27th after a furious cannonading for hours by the enemy he made a general advance in heavy

us an opportunity to meet between
the lines and do a little trading in the
way of coffee, tobacco, knives, newspapers, etc., and we would play cards
with them for several hours."
Confederate Veteran 15 (December
1907), 539.

Robt. D. Bond

98. The June 27 battle on Kenesaw Mountain took place on a stifling hot day with the temperature reaching as high as one hundred degrees. The Federals suffered a bloody repulse, but Union losses on Cleburne's front were closer to three hundred than the one thousand estimated by Bevens. See note 100 below.

99. Several people recorded this incident, although Colonel Martin's exact words were remembered variously. Confederate Maj. Gen. Samuel Gibbs French reported that Martin, after waving a white handkerchief tied to the end of a ramrod, shouted, "Come and remove your wounded; they are burning to death. We won't fire a gun until you get them away. Be quick!" Billy Barnes, who attributed the effectiveness of the Confederate defense to its devastating artillery fire, recalled Martin saying, "Boys, this is butchery." Martin then mounted the breastworks, waved his handkerchief, and called out to both lines, "Cease firing and help get out those men." Whatever Martin's exact words, Col. John I. Smith, Thirty-first Indiana Infantry, was so impressed by the act that he came forward to present the rebel with "a brace of fine pistols." Samuel G. French, *Two Wars: an Autobiography* (Nashville: Confederate Veteran, 1901), 211; *Confederate Veteran* 19 (May 1911), 206–07; 25 (April 1917), 168; 30 (February 1922), 49.

columns. Their assault in seven lines deep was vigorous and persistent on Cheatham's and Cleburne's Divisions of Hardee's Corps, the Confederates being covered by strong rifle pits which could not be carried by front attack, cooly and rapidly pouring a murderous fire into the massed Federals, causing losses entirely out of proportion to those inflicted upon the Confederates. The loss of the enemy in front of Cleburne's Division was one thousand deaths.[98] After the repulse of the second desperate assault the dry leaves and undergrowth in the forest before Cleburne's Division were set on fire by the shells and gun wadding, and began burning rapidly around the Federal wounded and dead, exposing them to a horrible death. This danger was observed by the Confederates who were ordered instantly to cease firing and Lieutenant Colonel Martin, First Arkansas Regiment of Cleburne's Division, called to the Federals that as an act of humanity his men would suspend further battle until the assailants could carry off their dead and wounded who were liable to be burned alive. This offer was accepted by the Federals and in this work of mercy the Federals were joined by the Confederates who leaped their head logs and helped to carry off their dead and wounded. This occurrence is perhaps unparalleled in the annals of war.[99] In this great struggle the Federal army numbered about or over one hundred thousand and

100. Casualties at Kenesaw Mountain have inspired an unusual amount of debate. The Federal loss was probably 1,999 dead and wounded, with another 52 reported missing. The Confederates lost 270 dead and wounded and 172 missing. Cleburne's division lost only 2 dead and 9 wounded. Lt. Allie T. Walthall died in skirmishing that followed the main battle. Purdue, *Pat Cleburne*, 333–35; Nichols and Abbott, eds., "Reminiscences of Confederate Service," 68. Both Cleburne and Johnston insisted that Federal losses were higher. See Connelly, *Autumn of Glory*, 359; Govan and Livingood, *A Different Valor*, 295. The figures used here, as for most of the casualty figures given in these notes, are from Mark M. Boatner, *The Civil War Dictionary*, rev. ed. (New York: David McKay Company, 1988).

101. Johnston's army began to withdraw under cover of night from Kenesaw Mountain on July 2, although skirmishing continued over the next several days. The army did not cross the Chattahoochie River on July 5, but it did entrench along its northern bank. The crossing came on July 8–9, after which the army fell back to entrenchments about three miles north of Atlanta. During the crossing, Polk's brigade served, as it had on so many previous occasions, as a rear guard for Hardee's corps. Purdue, *Pat Cleburne*, 336–38; Connelly, *Autumn of Glory*, 391–98; OR, vol. 38, pt. 5, 872–73.

Confederates numbered fifty thousand and in this Kennesaw battle our loss was eight hundred and eight and the Federal loss about five thousand.[100]

July 4th was celebrated by skirmishing all day. Sherman hoped to catch us and administer a fatal blow before we could cross the Chattahoochee, but we threw up strong intrenchments so quickly, and guarded the rear so skillfully that the army was all across the river July 5th without having been molested.[101]

But speaking of the Fourth of July. At this time Colonel Fellows, who had been with our command on our first trip to Richmond, was in prison at Johnson's Island together with about three thousand other officers. The rebels gained permission for Colonel Fellows to speak on the stand used by the guards as a watch tower. As he poured forth his thoughts, turning the Fourth of July to the glory of the South even the Yankee guards, who had stopped to listen were spellbound by his eloquence. He had it all his own way and the rebels were shouting like mad. The officer of the day finally awoke to the situation, took a file of soldiers, and brought the speech to a close. At another time in the same prison Lincoln's Proclamation was read, offering pardon and freedom to all rebel prisoners who would take the oath of allegiance. The officers lined up in the barracks and announced that any man who wished to

102. John R. Fellows had been captured at Port Hudson, Louisiana, while serving as a staff officer for Brig. Gen. William N. R. Beall, in July 1863. He was imprisoned at both Johnson's Island, Ohio, and Fort Delaware, on Pea Patch Island in the Delaware River, a mile from Delaware City. At both places, he earned a reputation as an orator, and he admitted that he "used to harangue" his fellow prisoners and encourage them to remain loyal to the Confederate cause. Fellows was also an excellent singer who led the prisoners' glee club on Johnson's Island. He was ultimately released from Fort Delaware on June 10, 1865. *Confederate Veteran* 5 (March 1897), 119, (October 1897), 514.

Johnson's Island sat in Sandusky Bay of Lake Erie, about a mile from the mainland. It opened in February 1862 and was originally designed to hold one thousand prisoners on its three hundred acres. Eventually, three thousand men were packed onto the island, most of them Confederate officers.

103. Thomas Shannon Logan, born about 1844 in Arkansas, was working as a clerk when the war started. According to the census of 1860, he lived with the family of his brother, Alexander H. Logan, a farmer and the sheriff of Jackson County. Logan had achieved the rank of corporal by the summer of 1863. He was captured at Nashville on December 16, 1864, and imprisoned at Camp Douglas, Illinois, where he remained until paroled on June 19, 1865. The Union general to whom he was related was John Alexander "Black Jack" Logan of Illinois. Service Records, Roll 49.

take the oath might step over to this line, give his name and be free. When Colonel Fellows was called he made a five minute talk in which he declared death was preferable.[102] One of our boys, Shannon Logan of Co. G, First Arkansas Regiment, eighteen years old, was captured. He was a relative of General Logan and when his name appeared General Logan's family drove down to the prison with the papers necessary for his release. They asked to see him and were shown a dirty, greasy, lousy private. Through the grime they recognized a fine boy with a noble face. They took him home, bathed him, clothed him, fed him, then told him to be their boy thenceforth. If this lonely boy, away from home, away from comrades had taken the oath he would have been free, with loving kinsmen, with luxury and riches, but he said "No, no! I will die first." So for him it was back to the filthy prison among the vermin and rats.[103]

This, one of the many instances of the loyalty displayed by the rank and file, should be told to coming generations that they may know how the Southern private never faltered, but was true to the core.

104. Leonidas Steadman (1838–1922), not mentioned in the text, was born in North Carolina. His family moved to Jacksonport in 1861, just in time for Steadman to join the Jackson Guards as a private. He returned to Jackson County after the war and married Alice Granada in 1866. They had six children. He eventually moved to Paragould, Arkansas, where he died. *Confederate Veteran* 30 (August 1922), 308.

Lon Steadman[104]

1. Bevens here gives yet another date for the crossing of the Chattahoochee, but as indicated in chapter 2, note 101, the correct dates are July 8–9.

The battle of Peach Tree Creek (July 20) found the Confederates on the offensive, and Gen. John Bell Hood, who had replaced Joseph Eggleston Johnston as commander of the Army of Tennessee on July 17, "lost heavily" (2,500 dead and wounded), as Bevens says. The First Arkansas, which had been held in reserve, was about to be thrown into battle when Maj. Gen. Patrick R. Cleburne was urgently directed to withdraw his men several miles to the southeast to reinforce Maj. Gen. Joseph Wheeler's cavalry, engaged in heavy skirmishing for control of an eminence known as Bald Hill. Cleburne marched his men south through Atlanta and then turned east toward Bald Hill. They bivouacked on the edge of the city for two hours before continuing the march. They joined Wheeler at daybreak on July 21, about two miles east of Atlanta. Cleburne described the ensuing skirmishing as the "bitterest" fighting of his life. The division suffered about three hundred casualties, but the Federals lost seven hundred men. Corps commander Hardee believed that without Cleburne's "timely arrival on the right, the enemy would on the morning of the 21st have succeeded in gaining the inner works of Atlanta." It was probably here that Capt. Samuel Shoup received his wound. Thomas L. Connelly, *Autumn of Glory: The Army of Tennessee, 1862–1865* (Baton Rouge:

Louisiana State University Press, 1971), 439–45; Howell and Elizabeth Purdue, *Pat Cleburne: Confederate General* (Hillsboro, Tex.: Hill Jr. College Press, 1973), 346–50; *The War of the Rebellion: A Compilation of the Official Records of the Union and Confederate Armies,* 70 vols. in 128 books and index (Washington: Government Printing Office, 1880–1901), ser. 1, vol. 38, pt. 3, 698–99 (cited hereafter as OR, and, unless otherwise indicated, all references are to Series 1).

2. Cleburne's division withdrew from Bald Hill, leaving it to the Federals, commanded by Brig. Gen. Mortimer Dormer Leggett, on the evening of July 21. Cleburne's men marched back to fortifications on the edge of Atlanta where they were joined by the remainder of the corps as it fell back from Peach Tree Creek. Just before daybreak on July 22, the march continued southeastward to Cobb's Mill, about three miles below the left flank of the Federal lines and about six miles southeast of Atlanta. They fell into line of battle after receiving twenty additional rounds of ammunition and enjoying a two-hour rest, but they were still in an exhausted condition. They had fought all day on July 21 in extremely hot weather, and they had been marching steadily since then. Now they marched back toward the northeast and prepared to strike at Maj. Gen. James Birdseye McPherson's exposed left flank to the southeast of the city in what would be called the battle of Atlanta. Purdue, *Pat Cleburne,* 350–51.

Chapter Three

JULY 12th we crossed the Chattahoochee near Atlanta. July 18th we marched four miles and built breastworks. July 20th there was hard fighting at Peach Tree Creek in which we lost heavily. Our noble Captain Shoup was wounded and the command devolved upon Second Lieutenant Clay Lowe. He and John R. Loftin were the only commissioned officers we had left.[1]

July 22 we marched ten miles to the right of Atlanta. Hardee had attacked the enemy in the rear and there had been a terrible struggle which lasted for hours. Toward evening we heard the Yankee Bands playing and the soldiers shooting and cheering and we knew they had won.[2]

While Johnston was in command he had preserved

3. Many soldiers in the army were angered by the removal of the popular Johnston. See also Sam R. Watkins, *"Co. Aytch": A Side Show of the Big Show* (New York: Collier Books, 1962), 172, 179; James L. Nichols and Frank Abbott, eds., "Reminiscences of Confederate Service by Wiley A. Washburn," *Arkansas Historical Quarterly,* 35 (Spring 1976), 69.

his army, and inflicted upon the enemy a loss almost equal to our strength when we began the campaign. Our loss had been about nine thousand, which had been filled by the return of the wounded and furloughed men, so that General Hood received an army fully as strong as it was at Dalton. We were as ready to fight as ever although certainly disappointed at the loss of Johnston. We felt that no other general could do what he had done.[3]

Soon after the war ended Johnston was going from Memphis to St. Louis. General Sherman and his staff were on their way to New Orleans. When Sherman learned that his former adversary was on board a certain boat he took passage for St. Louis on the same vessel. After supper he asked Johnston if he had any objection to going over with him the retreat from Dalton. Johnston said he had not. So Sherman spread his maps on the cabin table and, surrounded by a throng of listeners, they began. Sherman would ask about his line at a certain place, and Johnston would explain how his move was made. Sherman would point to his map and say: "How in the world did you get away from me here?" They talked all night. Johnston needed no map. He had been in the very thick of battle for seventy-four days; the map of campaign was burned into his brain, and he knew every foot of the ground. His retreat was a wonder to

4. This meeting between William Tecumseh Sherman and Johnston is recorded nowhere else, but it rings true, for each man admired the other. Johnston called Sherman "the genius of the Federal army," and he would catch his death of cold while serving as an honorary pallbearer at Sherman's funeral in 1891. Gilbert E. Govan and James W. Livingood, *A Different Valor: The Story of General Joseph E. Johnston,* *C.S.A.* (Indianapolis: Bobbs-Merrill Company, 1956), 393–94, 397–98.

5. Sgt. James M. Hensley, a painter by trade, enlisted as a twenty-year-old private in Company G. He had been wounded at Ringgold Gap. Compiled Service Records of Confederate Soldiers Who Served in Organizations from the State of Arkansas, National Archives Microcopy No. 317, Roll 48 (cited hereafter as Service Records).

Sherman and to the world. Yet this great military genius was thrown out on the eve of his final and greatest assault upon Sherman. An assault which would have saved Atlanta to the Confederacy. Hood and Davis tactics prevailed after that and the splendid, unconquered army was swept off the earth into the grave.[4]

Hood questioned the morale of his army, but as for that, our poor little Company G went into line under Hood as true as it ever had under Johnston. We fought for the cause, not the general. Jim Hensley, a boy who had been wounded severely, returned to the company.[5] His physician had not reported him for duty, but had given him merely a pass to his command. I was in the field hospital when the order to [move] forward was given. Hensley came to me saying: "Here, my dear old friend, is a little silver watch I wish to give you, for I shall be killed today."

I told him he had not been reported for duty; that he was still far from well, and begged him not to go into battle, especially as he had a presentiment that he should be killed. He turned his soulful eyes upon me. "Will, do you think I am afraid because I know I am going to be killed?" Putting his hand on his breast he continued, "I have no fear of death. I am a Christian, and I know I shall be safe in heaven." With tears we parted. He joined his brave comrades, Jim Murphy,

6. James H. Murphy is listed in Bevens's roster of Company G as a private who was discharged, possibly because of severe wounds, but Murphy's name does not appear on the company's surviving muster rolls. Four Murphys served in Company G, but none was named James, and only one, John M. Murphy, was still with the regiment by July 1864. His record does not indicate that he was wounded at Atlanta, but it does show that he was captured in the withdrawal to Jonesboro on September 1, 1864. Service Records, Roll 50. There was a James Murphy, born in 1825, who married Martha Ann Elizabeth McWhirter in 1857 in Jackson County. Ardith Olene Foster, *Marriage and Divorce Records of Jackson County, Arkansas, 1831–1875* (Newport, Ark.: Morgan Books, 1980), 78.

John Baird and George Thomas on the left of Company G, after the line was in motion.[6] They were moving against strong entrenchments heavily defended by abatis. These four boys saw they could crawl under the abatis without being seen and get close to the breastworks. After they started, the command was given to oblique to the left, but in the roar of the musketry the boys failed to hear it and went on alone. There were about a hundred Yankees on the breastworks watching our line which was advancing upon their rear. The four boys crawled close in, prepared, and opened up. At the first fire down came four Yankees. They were taken by surprise, not knowing there were any men at their front. The boys kept at their game until the Yankees ran. Then went forward to take possession of the works. Then they found themselves alone and two hundred of the enemy entrenched behind a second line! It was death anyway, so they ran forward firing on the troops with terrible accuracy. One man had a bead on Thomas when Murphy shot the fellow. One hinged for Murphy when Thomas bayoneted him. So they had it—hand to hand. Poor Hensley was killed, Murphy terribly wounded, Baird wounded, but Thomas would not surrender. He bayoneted them until they took his gun, then he kicked and bit until they finally killed him there. Four men had

7. Bevens here describes some of the action in the battle of Atlanta (July 22). In the bigger picture, Gen. Daniel Govan's brigade formed the right flank of the division, and the First and Fifteenth Arkansas, once again under the command of Col. John Colquitt, formed the left flank of the brigade. The advance, which began at 11:40 A.M., carried the brigade through "dense and almost impassable undergrowth." Much of the fighting took place on the slopes of Bald Hill, which the Confederates had abandoned the previous evening, and which the Federals now called Leggett's Hill. The First Arkansas led the attack nearly all day. It distinguished itself by successfully storming McPherson's "formidable entrenchments" and helping to capture two Union cannon and forcing the surrender of the Sixteenth Ohio Infantry. General Govan praised the regiment by saying, "The whole affair was gallantly, brilliantly executed, and has never been excelled in dash and spirit by any previous action of these veteran soldiers. . . . Indeed, I can scarcely conceive how the left . . . succeeded in gaining the works under the murderous fire to which they were exposed." Then, aware of the ferocious fighting carried on by groups of men like Baird, Hensley, Murphy, and Thomas, Govan continued, "In some places the enemy were bayoneted in their trenches, so stubbornly did they resist my little band." The weary Confederates fell back at nightfall. Connelly, *Autumn of Glory,*

445–50; Purdue, *Pat Cleburne,* 351–62; OR, vol. 38, pt. 3, 737–41.

8. The First and Fifteenth Arkansas lost Colonel Colquitt and Col. William Martin to wounds; Colonel Colquitt's wound eventually required amputation of his left foot. The regiment lost 15 dead, 67 wounded, and three missing—59 percent of the 144 men who entered the battle. The brigade as a whole lost about half of its one thousand men.

9. Following the battle of Ezra Church (July 28), in which the First Arkansas did not participate, Atlanta fell under a month-long siege. Govan's brigade bivouacked at several places on the outskirts of the city during those weeks. On August 30, Cleburne's division moved three miles to a ridge south of East Point, between the Macon & Western Railroad and the Atlanta and West Point Railway, its mission being to thwart a Union advance against the Macon & Western.

By the end of July, the army had again been reorganized. The First Arkansas remained in Hardee's corps, Cleburne's division, and Govan's brigade, and it remained consolidated with the Fifteenth Arkansas, but Govan's brigade had been turned into a nearly all Arkansas unit. This change had been made informally as Cleburne's division withdrew from Bald Hill on July 21. The reassignments were made official on July 31. The brigade, which now numbered only 534 men, also included the Second and Twenty-fourth Arkansas

killed twenty-five Yankees, but only one of the four lived to tell the tale. To question the morale of such men is farcical. The battle on our left raged all day, and we were defeated.[7] Our colonel lost his foot. One third of our regiment was gone. Great numbers were killed and wounded but the troops were as loyal and fought as bravely as any army on earth. This was Hood's second defeat. In two battles, he had lost ten thousand men—more than we had lost in the whole campaign, in seventy-four days' battles and skirmishes. It would not take long with such tactics to wipe out the rebel army.[8]

July 29th we marched back to Atlanta.[9] August 31st we marched to Jonesboro and on September 1st we moved to the right, threw up temporary works and Hardee's corps fought the Battle of Jonesboro. Hood's and Stewart's troops were at Atlanta, twenty miles away, and we were entirely unsupported. We fought all day against seven corps of Yankees. We were surrounded and fought in front and in the rear. Fought as General Cleburne always fought. The Yankees charged our company seven lines deep, but our thin line held firm until some of the boys happened to discover a line of Infantry charging in the rear. Then they began to waver. Our Lieutenant Commander Clay jumped on top of the breastworks, waved his gun, (the sixteen-shooter which the

(Consolidated), Fifth and Thirteenth Arkansas (Consolidated), Sixth and Seventh Arkansas (Consolidated), Eighth and Nineteenth Arkansas (Consolidated), and Third Confederate Infantry. Capt. Felix G. Lusk, formerly of Company K, now commanded the First and Fifteenth Arkansas, although he would soon be replaced by Capt. A. C. Hockersmith. OR, vol. 38, pt. 3, 662.

Ben Adler

10. If Bevens really intends to say a "sixteen-shooter," he must be referring to a repeating rifle. The Henry rifle was the only one of these weapons that could hold sixteen rounds (fifteen in the magazine, one in the breech), but it was manufactured in Connecticut. Very few of these weapons fell into Confederate hands. Alternately, and more likely, Bevens means to say "six-shooter," which could refer to any one of several types of revolver.

11. The battle of Jonesboro was the last battle for the control of Atlanta. Cleburne's division first attacked the Federals on August 31, but the movement was ill coordinated, with Cleburne attacking prematurely. The Confederates withdrew after a brief encounter with the enemy. On September 1, the Federals took the initiative. Cleburne's men were positioned on the right of Hardee's corps, with Govan's brigade holding a salient in the center of the brigade's line. Govan's men were nearly destroyed by a double envelopment when attacked by three Federal divisions.

Commander Clay refers to Lt. Henry Clay Lowe. Still, Hardee's corps held long enough for Lt. General Stephen Dill Lee's corps to withdraw and for Hood's army to begin its evacuation of Atlanta. Purdue, *Pat Cleburne*, 368–81; OR, vol. 38, pt. 1, 676, pt. 3, 726–30, 741–43. For a view of the fighting from Company H see Nichols and Abbott, eds., "Reminiscences of Confederate Service," 74–76.

12. There is no evidence to support Bevens's contention that Hardee had been offered command of the army before it was given to General Hood. It is true that Robert E. Lee had recommended Hardee over Hood to Jefferson Davis, but Davis did not offer the post to Hardee. Nathaniel C. Hughes, Jr., *General William J. Hardee, Old Reliable* (Baton Rouge: Louisiana State University Press, 1965), 215–17.

13. The Federals lost 1,453 men during the two days. The Confederates lost at least 2,636, but only Cleburne's casualties are known for September 1. 600 men in General Govan's brigade were captured, including Govan, although he was exchanged a week later. Additionally, his brigade had 26 men killed and 68 wounded. The First Arkansas suffered the further humiliation, not mentioned by Bevens, of having its regimental flag captured by the Fourteenth Michigan Infantry. This was not the original regimental flag presented to the Jackson Guards in May 1861 and later donated to the Confederate Museum by Mrs. Cockle (see chapter 1, note 24). The regiments of the Army of Tennessee received new battle flags in the spring of 1864, and it was this banner that fell at Jonesboro. It was returned to Arkansas in 1905 and is now on display at the Old State House in Little Rock. John C. Hammock, *With Honor Untarnished: The Story of the First Arkansas Infantry Regiment, Confederate States Army* (Little Rock: Pioneer Press, 1961), 119–20; Howard Michael Madaus and Robert D. Needham, *The Battle Flags of the Confederate Army of Tennessee* (Milwaukee: Milwaukee Public Museum, 1976), 21, 91–92.

officers of our company carried instead of sabres,)[10] and called to his men to stand their ground. He was on the breastworks but a few minutes when he fell, pierced through by one of the thousand bullets fired at him. As he fell he saw for the first time why his men wavered. He ordered a hasty retreat to the right, and although dreadfully wounded successfully threw the line of battle to the rear. He fell in my arms and I got him to an ambulance and sent him to a hospital. In Macon we had only one commissioned officer left, John R. Loftin.[11]

We would have been eaten up entirely, but for the coming of night, which gave Hardee a chance to unite his corps and throw up intrenchments. He displayed fine generalship throughout this engagement. Hardee had been offered the command of the army in Tennessee before Hood took it but had replied: "General Johnston is the only man able to command this army, and I will not have it."[12] Here was another terrible defeat for the new leader. Our loss at Jonesboro was about 2,500 men. The Yanks put our captured men on the train and sent them back over the old route.[13] The fort at Dalton was garrisoned by negro troops. A great number of these negroes were at the station when the prisoners arrived. They insulted our men, and tried to take them from the train, yelling, "No quarter, if we get you on the

14. I have been unable to verify this incident, although there were black Federal troops (Forty-fourth U.S. Colored Regiment) at Dalton.

15. The First Arkansas had withdrawn to Lovejoy's Station on the Macon & Western Railroad, forty miles by rail from Atlanta, on the morning of September 2.

16. Sherman issued his evacuation order on September 8 through the mayor of Atlanta, James M. Calhoun. It required that all Confederate civilians leave the city. People had a choice of going either north or south, and they could take whatever moveable property, including slaves, they desired. Sherman would supply transportation for those going south only as far as Rough and Ready, Georgia, about seven miles outside Atlanta. General Hood was expected to handle transportation arrangements beyond that point. Hood, of course, was outraged, and the massive eviction, which included 705 adults and 860 children, was not always as bravely endured as Bevens suggests. Richard M. McMurry, *John Bell Hood and the War of Southern Independence* (Lexington: University of Kentucky Press, 1982), 157; Franklin M. Garrett, *Atlanta and Environs: A Chronicle of Its People and Events,* 3 vols. (1954; Athens: University of Georgia Press, 1969–87), I, 636–43.

field." If white troops had not come to protect them there would have been serious trouble.[14]

Our corps camped on the Macon road.[15] It was a dark night and was raining heavily. By the flashes of lightning we saw the train of army ambulances coming out of Atlanta, and we heard female voices singing Dixie and other Southern songs. These were brave women, non-combatants, driven from their homes, by the infamous order of Sherman. They had no shelter, no provision and only the clothes they wore. Some bore nursing babes and one woman gave birth to a Dixie boy in the wagon train. Yet these glorious women would not show anguish or cry out to please the demon general. They shouted for Dixie and sang on their dreary ride. They went further South out of range of the beast of a general. He burned Atlanta and made war on women and children for the rest of the way on his infamous "march to the sea." As long as he had Johnston to fight he had no time for his diabolical deeds.[16]

September 12th we marched to Palmetto and camped there, and President Davis came to review his thrice defeated army. Beforehand a general order was read, that no cheers should be given on this review. Never-the-less, when Davis reached the center of the troops every man on the field joined in one mighty volume of sound, "Hurrah for General

17. The army marched to Palmetto, Georgia, about twenty miles west of Lovejoy's Station and twenty-five miles southwest of Atlanta, on September 18, not September 12. President Davis arrived on September 25 to review the army and to quell bickering within the Army of Tennessee's high command, particularly between Hood and Hardee. Davis left on September 27. A member of Company H also recalled the army's enthusiastic demonstration on behalf of Joe Johnston: "The next day [after the demonstration] orderlys and staff officers came down the line and said for us not to yell Johnstone and make Hood and Jeff feel bad, but lord they loved Joe to[o] well, and such a shout as they gave for him was long to be remembered." Steven E. Woodworth, *Jefferson Davis and his Generals: The Failure of Confederate Command in the West* (Lawrence: University Press of Kansas, 1990), 290–93; Nichols and Abbott, eds., "Reminiscences of Confederate Service," 73–74.

One private summarized the morale of Company G when he wrote to his father from Palmetto, "We are in a camp resting now which the boys needs very much. . . . The rest of the boys are all looking very well but they are dirty & look black but are washing up again. . . . The boys are well or at least all of us that are left as we have had a hard time of it in this campaign." John A. McDonald to Alvin McDonald, 28 September 1864, in "Civil War Letter of John A. McDonald," *Stream of History* 2 (October 1964), 11.

Johnston." They knew it would be impossible to court-martial the entire army.[17]

October 1st we crossed the Chattahoochee river at Moore Bridge. October 9th we crossed the Talacatacline river and went up the railroad as far as Dalton held by the negroes who had promised "no quarter" to our boys. General Cheatham detailed our brigade to guard the wagon train through a different route about four miles from Dalton, while he took Granberry's Brigade and our Texas troops to attack the fort. As we fought side by side in so many hard battles the Texas men asked that the Arkansas regiment (not on the ground) should have the honor of charging the fort, and this General Cheatham promised. He surrounded the fort and demanded its surrender. This was refused. While the artillery made ready the Texans passed the word down the line as though it came from General Cheatham, "Kill every damn one of them," which would have been carrying out their own threat of "no quarter." However, they saved their necks by five minutes, for when the white officers saw they were overwhelmingly surrounded they gave up. The prisoners were put to work at tearing up the railroad track. One of the negroes protested against the work as he was a sergeant. When he had paid the penalty for disobeying orders the rest tore up the road readily and

18. The army left Palmetto on September 29 as it embarked on the Franklin-Nashville campaign, which would continue into January 1865. The army swung around Atlanta to the northwest and then moved north to disrupt Sherman's supply line on the Chattanooga-Atlanta Railroad. It crossed the Chattahoochee on September 29–30 at Moore's Ferry. Just prior to leaving, General Hood had replaced Hardee, with whom he had been feuding for months, with Maj. Gen. Benjamin Franklin Cheatham (1820–86). Raids on Sherman's communication began on October 1. Connelly, *Autumn of Glory,* 470–82.

By October 8, Hood had moved nearly seventy miles northwest of Atlanta. The army crossed the Coosa River (which Bevens calls the Talacatacline) on October 9–10 and then swerved back to the northeast to seize the Western and Atlantic Railroad between Resaca and Dalton. The surrender of the Federal garrison at Dalton came on October 13. The Union commander, Col. Lewis Johnson of the Forty-fourth U.S. Colored Regiment, at first refused to surrender his nearly eight hundred men. He finally did so after light skirmishing, but, in the racially charged atmosphere described by Bevens, all Federal troops, and especially the black troops, were "immediately robbed and abused in a terrible manner." White officers were verbally abused, and at least six black soldiers were executed. OR, vol. 39, pt. 1, 717–23, 803–10; Christopher Losson, *Tennessee's Forgotten Warriors: Frank Cheatham and His Confederate Division* (Knoxville: University of Tennessee Press, 1989), 199–200.

rapidly. That evening the Texas command moved over to us. We heard them yelling and singing but we did not know what had happened. They were guarding the negro prisoners, and were calling to us, "Here are your 'no quarter' negroes, come and kill them!" The poor negroes, with eyes popped out nearly two inches, begged, prayed, and made all sorts of promises for the future. They soon moved on out of sight and the general turned them over to the engineering corps, where they did splendid service. This was better than killing them.[18]

That day as the wagons were in skirmish line ready for attack we heard firing in front of our advance column. Everything stopped and we made ready for action. Advancing, we discovered the cause of the tumult. A squad of scouts, whose captain was a man with long red hair, had given a great deal of trouble to the Yankees in that vicinity. Because he was an Independent Scout he had been outlawed and a price was placed upon his head. He and his outlaws were desperate fellows and accepted the "no quarter" clause. This squad was on our road and as it happened, met a squad of twenty-two Yankee scouts coming down the same road. The red-headed captain and his five men charged the superior squad, wounded six and killed four. The rest of the Yankees fled in haste. We were close upon them, so Red

19. I have been unable to verify this episode.

20. The itinerary given by Bevens mixes the pre-Dalton and post-Dalton marches. Cedar Town and Cave Spring were passed on October 8 and 9, respectively, with the Coosa River crossing, as noted above, on October 9 or 10. After the surrender of Dalton, the army first moved southward in hopes of drawing Sherman away from Atlanta. On October 15–16, Hood's army moved about nine miles south of LaFayette, Georgia; from there it marched, as Bevens says, to Center and Jacksonville, Alabama. From Jacksonville, the army turned abruptly northward on October 20 toward Gadsden, where it crossed the Coosa River once more to camp on Sand Mountain. Connelly, *Autumn of Glory*, 482–86; McMurry, *John Bell Hood*, 160–64; OR, vol. 39, pt. 1, 807–10; Purdue, *Pat Cleburne*, 389–90.

Head could not kill the wounded. He and his men took to the mountains and we never saw them again.[19]

We passed through Cedar Town and Cave Spring, and camped on Coosa river. We passed through Center and camped on Terrapin Creek. We crossed Chuckluck mountains and camped at Jacksonville. We crossed Coosa at Gadsden and camped on Sand mountain. We camped on Black Morgan river.[20]

On October 27th, we marched seven miles and camped in line around Decatur. It was a rainy night, so dark we could not see our file leader. If there were any roads we could not see them. It was impossible to finish the line of battle. The army had lost its way. I was standing beside the other boys holding to a small sapling when a new line came up, moving as best they could in a hog path, each man guessing at the way and calling to the man in front. A log about knee high lay across the path and I saw three different soldiers strike that log and fall over it into the muddy slash. Each time the man's gun went splashing ahead striking the fellow in front. There was cussin' all along the line. Finally we ran out on the log and warned others who came along, turning them safely around that point. On October 28th we went further in, completed the line and fought the Battle of Decatur. The night after the battle it turned

21. The army left the Sand Mountain region on October 22 with the intention of moving directly north to Guntersville, Alabama, and crossing the Tennessee River. However, Federal troop movements forced Hood to swerve westward to Decatur, Alabama. His army reached Decatur on October 26 to find it held by Federal forces. What Bevens calls the battle of Decatur was in fact brisk skirmishing on October 27–28 carried on by the divisions of General Cheatham and Maj. Gen. William Brimage Bate. Hood decided not to force a river crossing here either. He moved forty miles further west through freezing rain to Tuscumbia, Alabama, where a portion of his army crossed the Tennessee on October 30 and occupied Florence, Alabama. Purdue, *Pat Cleburne,* 389–90; McMurry, *John Bell Hood,* 164–65.

22. Cheatham's division, breaking off from the skirmishing at Decatur, joined the army at Tuscumbia on October 31 and made the river crossing, as Bevens states, on November 13. However, the division left Florence on November 21, not November 22. The official corps itinerary shows that the men then marched northward eighteen miles on November 22 and another fourteen miles on November 23 before arriving

at Waynesborough (not Warrenton). The corps then turned northeast, marching fourteen miles on November 24, eighteen miles on November 25 (when they would have passed through Henryville), and eighteen miles on November 26 (through Mount Pleasant) to within three miles of Columbia, Tennessee. Strangely, Bevens fails to mention the snow, freezing mist, and extremely cold weather the army endured on this march. "A bitter cold wind was whistling," recalled a Tennessee soldier, "and almost cut us in two." OR, vol. 45, pt. 1, 730; Losson, *Tennessee's Forgotten Warriors,* 202–03.

23. Brig. Gen. Gideon Johnson Pillow (1806–78) never held an important Confederate command after his shameful performance at Fort Donelson in February 1862. The estate referred to served as Pillow's home when he practiced law in Columbia before the war. He also owned a plantation in Arkansas, below Helena, but it had been ravaged by the Yankees. The *Atlanta Southern Confederacy* (7 August 1862, 2) reported that "a marauding band of Federal soldiers" had destroyed the plantation in July 1862. They also murdered the overseer, shot two Negroes who tried to hide from them, and carried off the other slaves.

so cold we nearly froze to death, but we did not mind marching over frozen ground.[21]

October 30th we marched thirty miles and passed Courtland, Alabama. On the 31st we marched twelve miles and camped at Tuscumbia. November 13th we crossed the Tennessee on a pontoon bridge at Florence. November 14th we built breastworks. On the 22nd we marched thirty-two miles and crossed the state line into Tennessee. On the 23rd we passed Warrenton [Waynesborough], the 25th through Henryville, and the 26th through Mount Pleasant.[22] We camped on General Pillow's place. He had a grand old Southern home. A fine brick mansion, surrounded by beautiful groves with splendid driveways. He had his own church, a comfortable and pretty brick building. These cultured people of the best blood of the South lived in this ideal spot and educated their children by teachers who lived in the home. Two members of this family, Ed Pillow and J. D. Pillow, live in Helena, where they still keep up the family customs and traditions.[23]

November 27th we marched nineteen miles and camped near Columbia. The enemy under Schofield had retreated from Mount Pleasant to Columbia and had entrenched in a formidable position. We went around them and crossing the Duck river on pontoon and rail bridges, we double-quicked to Spring

24. Maj. Gen. John McAllister Schofield (1831–1906) had about thirty thousand men just north of Columbia. By going "around them," Hood planned to move the bulk of his army (the corps of Cheatham and Lt. Gen. Alexander Peter Stewart) around the Federal left flank while moving the remainder of his troops against Schofield's front. Hood hoped that the pressure on Schofield's front would force the Federals to withdraw toward Nashville, thus allowing Cheatham and Stewart to strike the Federals between Columbia and Spring Hill (twelve miles northeast of Columbia).

25. Cheatham's corps, able to outpace the Federals, had gained Schofield's rear, but the slowness of Stewart's men to join in a coordinated strike on November 29 allowed the Federals to continue their withdrawal toward Franklin, about fourteen miles north of Spring Hill. Cleburne's division attacked the Federal right flank at 4:15 A.M. on November 29 and jolted it backward. Govan's brigade was positioned at the center of the division. Everyone, not just General Forrest (now a lieutenant general), who commanded Hood's cavalry, was frustrated by the failure to press on after a heavy Federal artillery barrage had briefly disrupted the Confederate advance. Cleburne was beside himself at Hood's refusal to press the attack after dark, an action that Federal officers confessed would have destroyed Schofield's army. For his part, Bevens's brigade commander, General Govan, insisted after the war, "Had we not been halted and instead made a determined advance, we could in 20 minutes have captured or destroyed [the corps of Maj. Gen. David Sloane] Stanley, together with 800 wagons and his artillery." Forrest, at least, was able to attack the Federal supply trains at Thompson's Station, two miles north of Spring Hill, that evening. Purdue, *Pat Cleburne,* 392–407; Losson, *Tennessee's Forgotten Warriors,* 203–17.

26. Dr. Brickie must be Dr. William C. Brickell, appointed surgeon in 1862. He served as senior surgeon in Cleburne's division while assigned to the Third Confederate Regiment. I have been unable to identify a surgeon named Gray in the Army of Tennessee. Joseph Jones, "Roster of the Medical Officers of the Army of Tennessee," *Southern Historical Society Papers* 22 (1894), 175.

Hill and engaged the enemy with Cleburne's Division.[24] Our regiment was one of the first in action, after the cavalry had skirmished with them. Night overtook us and we could not see to fight. Forrest wished to attack them, even in the night, but was not permitted. As their force was much superior to ours, it would have been useless. Hood did not think they would retreat, but at daylight, when he began to complete his line, surrounding them, he discovered that they had flown to Franklin! With muffled cannon, silently and swiftly, Schofield had fled through the night.[25]

Company G lost some good men at Spring Hill. We established a hospital there, with Dr. Brickie and Dr. Gray in charge to care for the wounded. We brought the ordnance from Columbia and followed the enemy.[26]

The Yankees had been reinforced and had entrenched at Franklin, behind the works they had built some months before. In front of their works was an open field with not a tree or ravine for a mile and a half. Just before the breastworks was an open ditch six feet wide and three feet deep. At the end of the ditch next to the breastworks, were placed poles sharpened spear-shape. Their main works were six feet at the base. The cannon-breast portion was cut down so that the guns, resting on oak logs, were on a

27. Park Marshall, a native of
Tennessee, was active in Confederate
affairs and wrote extensively about the
war. The excerpts Bevens provides
here were taken from an address published in the *Confederate Veteran* 20
(August 1912), 363.

level with our bodies. Behind the whole was a thicket of locust trees, as close together as they could possibly grow. After the battle these trees were found to have been cut off level with the breastworks by Confederate balls.

As a description of this battle of Franklin, November 30, 1864, I insert an extract from the Park Marshall address delivered forty-eight years afterward:[27]

"I was born at Franklin, and as a small boy I visited this battle field when the smoke had scarcely disappeared, and the impression of that morning is still in my memory. Without exaggeration I may say that the severest battle of modern history was fought on these plains. In the forefront of that battle there were not over 20,000 Union troops, not over 15,000 Confederates, yet the killed on one side was greater in two or three hours than occurred on any one day on one side in any other battle of the Civil War, except Antietam.

"All the generals objected to the charge. Forrest, the best cavalry leader in the South, begged Hood to change his murderous plan, saying, 'I know every hogpath in this county, and I can show you a route which will give us a chance.'

"The lesser generals entered their protest along with the great generals. Men of world-wide fame,

28. It is doubtful that these were Cleburne's last words, although they probably express his thoughts at the time. The fullest biography of Cleburne attributes several similar statements to the Irishman prior to the battle. When ordered by General Hood to drive the Federals from their defenses, Cleburne replied, "General, I will take the works or fall in the attempt." And General Govan recalled the scene as Cleburne issued final orders to his brigade commanders: "He seemed greatly depressed and fully realized, as did every officer present, the desperate nature of the assault we were about to make." Cleburne was accompanying Govan's brigade into battle when he fell. Purdue, *Pat Cleburne*, 419–20.

29. General Hood's frontal assault at the battle of Franklin, fought on November 30, 1864, had been strongly opposed by Cheatham and Forrest. It was a disaster. Cleburne's division was positioned in the center of the formation, east of the Columbia Pike. Hood lost 6,252 of 26,897 men, including 6, not 7, generals killed: Cleburne, John Adams, John Carpenter Carter, States Rights Gist, Hiram Bronson Granbury, and Otho French Strahl. Five other Confederate generals were wounded, and one was captured. Altogether, fifty-five Confederate field officers (majors and above) were reported killed, wounded, or missing at Franklin. OR, vol. 45, pt. 1, 684–86. For the battle generally see James Lee McDonough, *Five Tragic Hours: The Battle of Franklin* (Knoxville: University of Tennessee Press, 1983).

As the attack began, General Govan reportedly remarked to Cleburne, "I think, General, there will not be many of us who will get back to Arkansas." Cleburne replied, "Well, Govan, if we are to die, let us die like men." Purdue, *Pat Cleburne*, 420. A vivid description of the attack from the vantage point of Company H may be found in Nichols and Abbott, eds., "Reminiscences of Confederate Service," 81–84.

and privates too, had their opinion, but not the right to speak.

"To send soldiers against such a position was suicidal. Every man in the South available for service was in the field. When these men were killed the Confederacy was destroyed. Oh, for a Johnston before the fatal word was given! Against every protest Hood ordered the advance. What were Cleburne's last words to his noble warrior boys?

'Boys, we are ordered to charge the works. I don't think we can take them, but we can try. Forward!'[28]

"In thirty minutes this glorious patriot's blood was flowing upon the ground. The advance was made without a halt, but the men were mowed down as wheat before the reaper. They marched to the breast-works and scaled the walls, but they were bayoneted on top of the works and fell over on the enemy. Seven dead generals were brought and laid on this porch—Cleburne, Granberry, Strahl, Gist, Carter and Adams. Adams fell, leaving his dead horse on the very crest of the breastworks. Cleburne's horse fell also crossing the works. This is one of the most heroic pictures of the war."[29]

Sixty per cent of our army was killed and wounded. The enemy retreated to Nashville after the best day's work (for them) they had ever done.

Our company had but one officer left. We were

30. Bevens's estimate of 60 percent casualties is ridiculously high if he is referring to the fighting at Franklin (23 percent is nearer the mark), but everyone agreed it was a disaster for the Confederacy. Perhaps Bevens is suggesting the percentage of losses suffered by the army through the entire campaign. After the battle, Col. Peter V. Green commanded the consolidated First, Second, Fifth, Thirteenth, Fifteenth, and Twenty-fourth Arkansas regiments. The remainder of Govan's brigade consisted of the Sixth and Seventh Arkansas (Consolidated) and Eighth and Nineteenth Arkansas (Consolidated). Brig. Gen. James Argyle Smith replaced Cleburne as division commander. OR, vol. 45, pt. 1, 667. The itinerary for Cheatham's corps for December 1 reads: "To-day spent in burying the dead, caring for the wounded, and reorganizing the remains of our corps." OR, vol. 45, pt. 1, 731.

31. Cheatham's corps itinerary for December 2–14 shows that he advanced along the Nashville Pike to within five miles of Nashville. The next two weeks were spent skirmishing and building defenses. OR, vol. 45, pt. 1, 731. The battle of Nashville (December 15–16) found Hood's army halting a Union attack on December 15 but then falling back a few miles to reorganize. Cheatham's corps, which had begun the fight on the extreme Confederate right (with

Govan's brigade forming the division's left flank), was shifted on the evening of December 15 to the extreme left, which had borne the brunt of the first day's fighting. The next morning, Smith's division was pulled out of the line and assigned to the center of Hood's line, although Govan's brigade was sent almost immediately back to the left. Unfortunately, the report of Colonel Green, who assumed command of the brigade when Govan fell wounded, has been lost, so we do not know precisely what happened next. We do know, however, that when fighting resumed on December 16, Hood's line snapped, having been extended too far with too few men. Govan's brigade, for example, when sent back to the left, had been asked to defend a front originally assigned to the entire division. General Govan fell wounded with a bullet in his throat on December 16. The Federals reported casualties of 3,061 out of 49,773; Hood's losses are unknown, but his dead and wounded were relatively few, probably about 1,500. However, 4,462 Confederates, including 3 generals, were captured. Losson, *Tennessee's Forgotten Warriors*, 232–40; OR, vol. 45, pt. 1, 739–40.

32. Cheatham's corps withdrew to Franklin on the night of December 16. It continued on to Spring Hill on December 17 and arrived there that evening. No official reference to the incident described by Bevens can be found.

consolidated with Company B and the two together scarcely made a full company. The whole regiment was consolidated into six companies, instead of ten.[30]

The enemy's loss was slight compared with ours. The bravest of the blood of the South was poured out for nothing. Who was right, Johnston or Hood?

We followed Schofield to Nashville and invested that post, but we were outnumbered, as he had been re-inforced from every quarter. He broke our line and captured about half of our regiment. My friend, Bob Bond was captured; Logan too, and many others.[31]

We retreated in quick time. Near Spring Hill a squad of about fifty cavalrymen made a dash through our line, as we had stacked arms and were preparing to camp for the night, and went far to the rear. Coming along the pike, never dreaming of danger, were four soldiers, bearing a wounded man on a litter. The Yankee squad shot the doctor's horse, wounding the doctor and killed one of the four soldiers. As the poor fellow fell, the wounded man rolled out on the pike. The front line, recovered from its surprise, grabbed the guns, surrounded the Yankees, captured them and made things lively for them for awhile.[32]

We crossed the [Duck] river at Columbia on two pontoon bridges, one for Forrest's cavalry, being about two hundred yards below us, down the river.

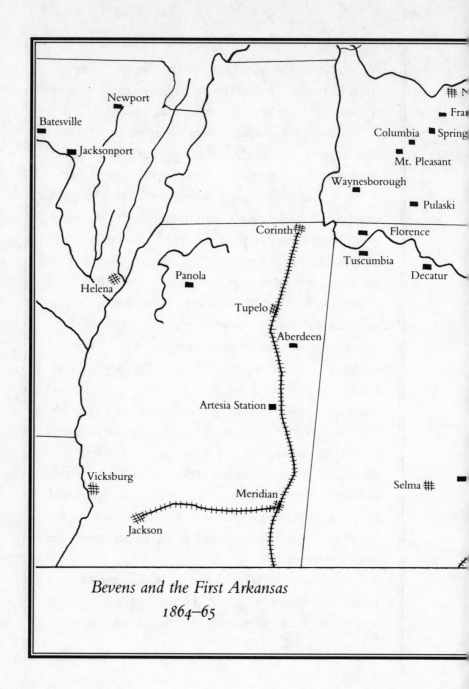

Newport

Batesville

Jacksonport

Helena

Panola

Corinth

Tupelo

Aberdeen

Artesia Station

Vicksburg

Meridian

Jackson

Mt. Pleasant

Columbia

Spring

Waynesborough

Pulaski

Florence

Tuscumbia

Decatur

Selma

Fra

Bevens and the First Arkansas
1864–65

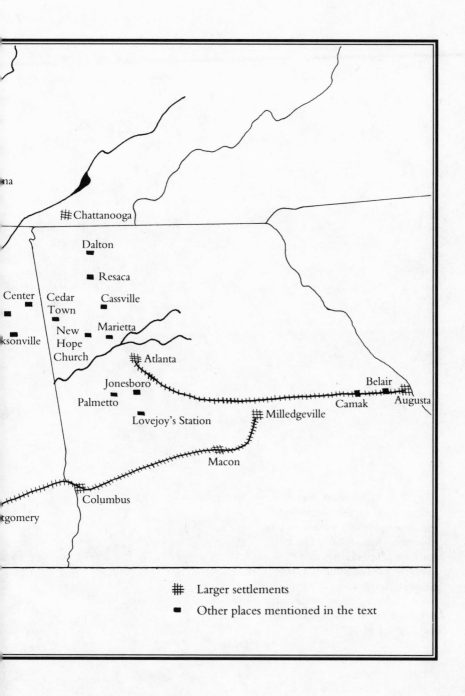

na

Chattanooga

Dalton

■ Resaca

Center   Cedar   Cassville
          Town
■
          New   ■ Marietta
ksonville Hope
          Church
                   ⌗ Atlanta
          Jonesboro
          ■   Belair
   Palmetto   Camak   ■   ⌗
          ■   Augusta
   Lovejoy's Station   ⌗ Milledgeville

                            ⌗
                          Macon

⌗ Columbus

tgomery

⌗   Larger settlements

■   Other places mentioned in the text

33. The corps crossed Duck River
on December 19. On December 18,
the corps had fought a skirmish about
two miles south of Spring Hill and
had bivouacked that night on the
south bank of Rutherford's Creek.
Skirmishing continued on the morning of December 19 before the corps
withdrew that afternoon to the river.
OR, vol. 45, pt. 1, 731.

It was almost dark, but skirmishing was still going on, when Forrest's pontoon broke loose, leaving him, his staff and about two hundred of his cavalry.[33]

Our ordnance was crossing on our bridge, and all was over except two wagons. Our regiment was waiting on the bank. General Cheatham and his staff were at the top of the bank. General Forrest rode up to our bridge and was about to cut off the three wagons of ordnance when the driver whipped up his horses to join the other wagons. Forrest took his pistol and threatened to kill him if he attempted to go on the bridge ahead of the cavalry. The driver was quite plucky. He said his orders were to follow the ordnance train; if General Forrest did not like it he must go to higher officers. Forrest was furious. He spurred his horse and went to General Cheatham, swearing he would cross that bridge ahead of the ordnance. General Cheatham was perfectly calm, and explained that he wished to get the wagons over before night, and into camp, so he could lay hands on his ordnance. Forrest was not pacified. He drew his pistol and threatened to shoot Cheatham, who rode to him at once, saying, "Shoot; I am not afraid of any man in the Confederacy."

The infantry with loaded guns, closed in around them, prepared to defend Cheatham. The cavalrymen, who had not heard what was said, came up the

34. The incident involving Cheatham and Forrest occurred essentially as Bevens describes it. However, it seems that Cheatham did not remain as cool as Bevens portrays him, and one report says it was corps commander Stephen Dill Lee, not Forrest's adjutant, who stepped between them and "pacified the chafing Cheatham." Another witness says that the two generals apologized on the spot, but reports are mixed as to which command eventually crossed the bridge first. Losson, *Tennessee's Forgotten Warriors,* 240. Stephen Lee's biographer does not mention his man being involved in this incident, but Lee had been wounded in the foot during a skirmish just north of Spring Hill. His condition squares with the account of the witness who identifies Lee as the peacemaker. Herman Hattaway, *General Stephen D. Lee* (Jackson: University of Mississippi Press, 1976), 146–47.

35. Cheatham's corps arrived at Pulaski on December 21 after marching twenty-three miles southward from Columbia to Lynnville on December 20. A driving snowstorm hit the column on December 21 and added to the misery of thousands of Hood's men who marched without shoes. General Smith complained about the "ill-provided-for condition" of his division, "many being barefooted and otherwise badly clothed." Connelly, *Autumn of Glory,* 512; OR, vol. 45, pt. 1, 732, 740.

hill to see what was going on. Forrest's adjutant plunged between the two generals and pulled Forrest down toward the bridge. By that time the wagons were over. So General Forrest and his troops crossed the bridge without further parley. It might have been a terrible tragedy. If either general had been killed, we would have had war right there.

Next day Forrest sent an apology to Cheatham, at least so it was reported. The affair was witnessed by our company, but it was kept quiet as we had troubles enough without fighting each other. Forrest was a great officer and a fine cavalry leader, but he was tyrannical and hot-headed.[34]

December 20th we marched all day on the pike to Pulaski in a cold rain—a rain that froze on the trees. We had to sleep on the wet ground. Many men were barefooted and marched over the pike with bleeding feet.[35] We were called the "straggling squad" because we had to march more slowly than the others, and we were between the infantry and the rear cavalry, commanded by Forrest. In his mind a straggler deserved death. When he came up to a poor little squad he struck one, a Lieutenant, who was in charge of the barefoot squad, over the head with his sword and ordered him to go on and keep up with his command. He would listen to no excuse, as if these barefooted men, braving sleet and snow with bleeding

36. It is true that Nathan Forrest had a temper and was a strict disciplinarian, but men who knew him better than did Bevens took a more kindly view. Said one of Forrest's officers, "The men learned that General Forrest was not cruel, nor unnecessarily severe, but they also learned that he would not be trifled with." Quoted in Robert Selph Henry, *"First With the Most" Forrest* (Indianapolis: Bobbs-Merrill, 1944), 215.

37. Again Dr. Brickie is probably Dr. Brickell; Peter Green was still colonel of the regiment. Cleburne's division surgeon was Dr. D. A. Linthicum, appointed surgeon in 1862 and assigned to Cleburne's division in June 1863. Cleburne frequently praised Dr. Linthicum in official reports. Following the battle of Chickamauga, he wrote, "The completeness of his arrangements, his careful supervision of subordinates, both on the field under fire and elsewhere, and in the hospitals, secured our gallant wounded the prompt attention, and all comfort and alleviation of pain attainable in the exigencies of battle." Jones, "Roster of the Medical Officers of the Army of Tennessee," 229; OR, vol. 30, pt. 2, 158.

feet, were not doing their duty as loyally as any man in the army.[36]

These incidents are a part of the unwritten history; merely a few things that I know to be facts in our army life with Company G.

We established a hospital at Pulaski to care for our sick and wounded, and left it in charge of Dr. Brickie. I went to the Colonel of our regiment and told him I feared Dr. Brickie would detail me to be his druggist; that I wanted a pass so I could go on ahead and meet the command beyond the town. He gave it to me and I had gotten about half a mile beyond Pulaski, when I heard a horse galloping behind me. It was the Division Surgeon, Dr. L., who stopped me, saying, "Are you Bill Bevens of Company G, First Arkansas."[37]

"I am."

"I detailed you to report to Dr. Brickie, corps surgeon in charge of Corps Hospital at Pulaski."

"I won't do it."

"If you don't, I will have you court-martialed."

"All right, but I won't go."

After he rode away I thought more soberly. I had been in the army four years and had never been arrested. Perhaps I had better go. I went back, but I gave it to Dr. Brickie. I told him there were a hundred druggists in that army; why didn't he get some

38. Cheatham's corps left Pulaski
on December 22 to continue its
retreat southward. It crossed the
Tennessee River near Florence,
Alabama, on December 26 and continued the retreat toward Corinth,
Mississippi. OR, vol. 45, pt. 1, 732.

other one? He answered that he had selected me because he knew I would not drink his whiskey nor give it away to "bums," but keep it for the sick. I told him I would give away every spoonful of it. I told him it was all right for him to be captured. He would be paroled. But I should be sent to Johnson's Island to freeze.

He said he would arrange that. He knew all the assistant surgeons and told them when we were captured they must address me as "Doctor." He ordered Dr. Gray to take charge of Ward 4, but to call it my ward.

So the army went without me and I felt sad indeed. I had not been separated from my comrades before. But "It is not what you want that makes you fat, but what you have."[38]

Forrest's cavalry was the last to leave. High officers would call on Dr. Brickie, cough and say they were ill, hoping he would give them a drink. He was a positive man and all men looked alike to him. The reply was always, "Not a darned drop; it is for the sick and wounded." The cavalry surgeons would beg for some, but to no purpose, for they got the same answer.

The infantry had been gone four days. Some of our patients had been taken to the homes of the good Southern women, some had gone with the cavalry,

on horseback and in wagons. There was a big decrease in our hospital. About three o'clock in the afternoon Dr. Brickie told me I could go and gave me a pass. He added, "Here are ten plugs of tobacco; you can hire some of the cavalry fellows to let you ride, and you may keep up with them."

I left him with a glad heart, but I did not know what I was up against. A lone web-foot to keep up with Forrest's Cavalry! I was certainly used to hardships, but that was more than I could do, to save my life. I went over the muddy road until my wind was almost gone, and I had to rest. One of our boys belonging to Hardee's Guards, came along and spying me, rode up to where I was, saying, "Bill, is that you? You have too much baggage. Give me some of it, and I will deliver it to your regiment wagons when I get back to the army."

I unloaded, rested for an hour and struck out again. The cavalry was ahead of me. I moved faster, for a Yankee rear does sometimes hurry a fellow.

I went all night; slept in the road and at daylight started again, making a good day's march. Late in the evening I found I was near the cavalry again, so I made great strides to catch up. Ahead I saw a bridge across a stream and Forrest and his staff walking on the gravel bar. I hoped I could slip over before they saw me and handed the guard my pass. He said,

"You will have to show it to General Forrest." I was frightened sure enough. General Forrest did not care for passes or anything else when out of humor. I had faced a thousand Yankee guns, but I couldn't face Forrest!

I waited some distance off, hoping he would go to an other part of the line, but he seemed to attend to that bridge himself. Finally he did walk away a few paces. Then I ran up to the adjutant, showed him my pass, and he waved the guard to let me go over.

I tried to beat Forrest to the next bridge, but when I got there he was on the bank higher above it. By their firelight I could see the infantry across the river and I thought, "I am safe now." When I reached the pontoon bridge over the Tennessee, the cavalry was crossing. I started across in the dark, but the guard stopped me. "You can't cross here—pass or no pass— you will have to see General Forrest." I argued with that guard, but it did no good. Then I thought to myself, "He will not shoot into his own men," and I said, "I am going across and you may shoot me if you like." I ran past him. He could not see me in the dark, or he might have shot.

After I got across the bridge I found that my command had gone two days before, so I camped all night by the straggler's fire. It was one of the worst nights of the campaign. A biting cold wind was

39. Cheatham's men passed through Alabama and arrived at Corinth, Mississippi, on the evening of December 31. By the end of 1864, Company G had lost 102 of 143 men (the number whose service records have survived) to death, desertion, discharge, capture, and transfer. Twenty-three men had died, and one more would die in 1865. Forty-three men had been wounded.

blowing and we fairly froze to the ground. For two days I followed my regiment. My rations gave out and I was trudging along the road, forlorn and very hungry, when I heard some one call me. It was a boy of Company G, detailed with the engineers' corps. I stayed with him that night. He had plenty of grub and filled me up.

December 27th, we passed Tuscumbia and on the 29th we camped at Iuka. On this march we crossed Bear Creek on a railroad bridge. The mules were unhitched from the wagons and led across. When I got there a fine pair of mules were on the bridge. They got half way over, then mule-like, decided they would back a little, and they backed clear off the bridge and went under the water, head and ears, to the amusement of the web-foot soldiers.

January 1, 1865, we marched seven miles and camped near Corinth. Here we washed up, and felt of ourselves, to see if we were all there. Here I caught up with my command. I surely was glad to see the boys and they were to see me, for they supposed I was eating rats on Johnson's Island. There were not many of us left. The killed, wounded and captured at Nashville had about finished the "shooting-match."[39]

We traveled over the Mobile & Ohio railroad to Tupelo, from which place I was sent to Aberdeen to

229

40. Cheatham's corps spent nine days at Corinth before continuing the retreat to Tupelo, where it halted on January 13, 1865. That same day, Hood was replaced as commander of the Army of Tennessee by Lt. Gen. Richard Taylor. Losson, *Tennessee's Forgotten Warriors*, 242-44. Aberdeen, Mississippi, is located about thirty miles south of Tupelo, but Bevens must mean Artesia (rather than Alesia), which is another thirty miles south of Aberdeen on the rail line to Mobile. On January 20, Cheatham's and Stephen Lee's corps received orders to depart from Tupelo for Augusta, Georgia. Their ultimate destination would be South Carolina, where Gen. Joseph Eggleston Johnston was organizing an army to oppose William Tecumseh Sherman. Losson, *Tennessee's Forgotten Warriors*, 242–44; OR, vol. 45, pt. 2, 800, 802.

41. Confederate money was practically worthless by 1865. In March, one gold dollar was worth seventy dollars in Confederate script. Of course, prices fluctuated regionally, and in Mobile prices were not as high as they would have been in Richmond or New Orleans. Mobile happened to have a city ordinance against extortion by merchants. Emory M. Thomas, *The Confederate Nation: 1861–1865* (New York: Harper & Row, 1979), 284; E. Merton Coulter, *The Confederate States of America 1861–1865* (Baton Rouge: Louisiana State University Press, 1950), 234.

bring the medical wagons to Alesia, where they were to be put on cars and taken to South Carolina. At Richmond (while I was in Aberdeen) it was decided to give a furlough to seven men of every company, so we might visit our homes in Arkansas. The boys put my name in the hat and drew for me and I got it. The other boys who got furloughs left at Meridian to make their way to Arkansas. They meant to take chances at crossing the river to get home. I was waiting at the Alesia station to deliver my medical supplies. The officer who came to ship them said, "Isn't your name Bill Bevens?" I said, "Yes". "Well, you have a furlough for 120 days to go to Arkansas." I said, "You are wrong. I never applied for one. Never have had one. I have been with the army nearly four years and have never seen Arkansas in all that time."[40]

But as the train flew by, the boys yelled at me that I had a furlough; so I went to see about it. It was at the Eighth Arkansas headquarters and I had no authority to stop. I had to go to South Carolina before I could get it. My crowd went with me.

I went on with the army. At Mobile some of us went again to the Battle House restaurant. We ate three rations in one meal, and our bill was one hundred and twenty dollars. Our paper currency had taken a great fall.[41]

It was a cold ride down on the Mobile & Ohio

42. Milledgeville, Georgia's state capital with a population of only 2,480 in 1860, was badly battered by this stage of the war. Sherman's army had marched through the town a few months earlier. For conditions see James C. Bonner, *Milledgeville: Georgia's Antebellum Capital* (Athens: University of Georgia Press, 1978), 177–200, and T. Conn Bryan, *Confederate Georgia* (Athens: University of Georgia Press, 1953), 168–70.

43. Cheatham's corps arrived in Augusta, Georgia, on February 9. On February 10 it crossed the Savannah River into South Carolina and headed for Columbia. Bevens would have left soon afterward. After his departure, the army continued on to North Carolina, where it again saw action on March 19 at Bentonville. General Johnston had been given command of the army on February 22. His force, totaling only 21,000 men, held its own against Sherman on February 19, but withdrew to Smithfield following skirmishing on February 20–21. Reorganized at Smithfield, Johnston's army headed for Raleigh on April 10 and finally surrendered at Greensboro on April 27. At that time, the First Arkansas was commanded by Capt. William H. Scales, formerly of Company C (the Camden Knights, of Ouachita County), and had been consolidated with the Second, Fifth, Sixth, Seventh, Eighth, Thirteenth, and Fifteenth Arkansas regiments and Third Confederate Regiment under the command of Col. E. A. Howell. Colonel Green still commanded the brigade while General Govan contin-ued his convalescence. They still served in Hardee's corps, but Maj. Gen. John Calvin Brown commanded their division. Losson, *Tennessee's Forgotten Warriors*, 244–48; OR, vol. 47, pt. 1, 1061, 1106–1108, pt. 2, 1174.

railroad. The soldiers were thinly clad and few of them had shoes. One or two men froze, riding on top of the cars. We traveled to Milledgeville, Georgia, and from there we had to march over a forty mile gap to the Augusta road.[42] I found my friends, Ed Dickinson, Ben Adler and Thad Kinman were still in Augusta. They got me a new gray suit with a long tail coat. I sure was dressed in the height of style, but my shoes hardly corresponded to my suit. They were not very stylish.

In South Carolina I got my furlough, told my comrades good-bye, and took letters from them to the homefolks.[43]

General Cheatham was in a box car and I got on the same car. It was the first time I had seen him since the quarrel with Forrest. I told him I had a furlough and I wanted to get transportation. He seemed to doubt it and said, "Let me see your furlough." He looked at the signature and he knew it was genuine.

Securing transportation I went back to Augusta. I went out to Belair, ten miles from the city, where my uncle had a summer residence. He was very kind to me. Next morning we went into the city and found a great commotion. General Beauregard was placing all stragglers in the guard house. My uncle said, "Son, you go back to Belair and I will see General Beauregard about it. But I answered, "The general

44. The order issued by Gen. Pierre G. T. Beauregard concerning stragglers was intended to maintain law and order in Augusta. The city had been spared a visit by Sherman's army, but the morale of the citizens had been seriously damaged by a wave of lawlessness that began in November 1864. By mid-February 1865, when Bevens was in Augusta, stragglers and all variety of rogues and riffraff were robbing government stores and harassing the citizenry. The city's newspapers failed to mention the orders. They paid more attention to Sherman's occupation of Savannah. However, the press did express concern over the lawlessness. Prices in Augusta, while rising during Bevens's previous visit, were soaring by early 1865. Coffee was up to $35 per pound, pork $3.35 per pound, eggs $6.50 per dozen, and butter $10 per pound. Beauregard was in Augusta from February 1 to 10, before going to South Carolina. T. Harry Williams, *P. G. T. Beauregard, Napoleon in Gray* (Baton Rouge: Louisiana State University Press, 1955), 249–51; *Augusta Chronicle and Sentinel,* 1 February 1865, 3, 1 March 1865, 2.

45. Forty Mile Gap is not identified on any map. Bevens must be referring to the point west of Augusta to which he had marched from Milledgeville. Below, Bevens mentions passing General Walthall, and General Walthall was in the vicinity of Camak and Mayfield, Georgia, en route to Augusta between February 13 and 15.

46. This is the same General Walthall identified in chapter 2, note 93. Bevens refers to him as General Walthold in the original text.

will have you in the guard house if you go to bothering him. I have an authority that ranks him or any general, as it is by order of the war department."[44]

When we went back to Belair that night my uncle presented me with a fine pair of boots which cost $100. Then my stylish outfit was complete. I told them goodbye, went to see Ed Dickinson, Ben Adler and Thad Kinman, and left for home.

I got to Forty Mile Gap.[45] I had more baggage than when I went down. As I marched along one of the drivers of the four-mule wagons asked if I wanted to ride. A web-foot never refused. He said he would walk if I would ride and drive, but I told him I had never driven a four-mule team in my life.

"Oh, that's all right," said he, "the mules follow the wagon ahead without a driver."

I rode his mule and drove his wagon, stylishly dressed, as I have said, in my long-tailed coat and fine new boots. The Virginia soldiers going on foot to their command, guyed me greatly. "When the war is over I bet that fellow will never tell that he drove a wagon train." Then others would yell, "Don't that guy look fine with his gay clothes on!" General Walthall[46] came along and attracted by my dress, eyed me muchly. I did not know what was in my wagon, and to avoid inquiry, and trouble for the driver, I began to whip up the mules, looking the other way.

But that didn't work. The general called out authoritatively, "What have you, sir, in that wagon?"

"Quartermaster's supplies," I answered, hastening on. Soon I passed the danger line for myself and the driver and was safe from any general (except a Yankee General!)

I stayed with the driver until two o'clock in the morning, when I had to leave for Milledgeville, to be in time for the outgoing train. I got there ahead of time, and witnessed one of the sad trials of refugees. An old man and his daughter, a beautiful young girl, were apparently in great haste to get their baggage off on the train, and seemed relieved when they had stowed away the last package. They themselves were just getting on the train when two policemen arrested the old man and started back to town with him. There were eight or ten Arkansas and Texas soldiers on the train. They could not see a nice young girl driven off the cars, and her father treated like a criminal. When she began to cry the crisis had arrived. They jumped off with their guns and pistols and took the old man from the policemen, gave him a pistol, saying "kill them both, and we will bury them right here." The old man refused to shoot, but the policemen did not tarry, nor did they come back.

At Montgomery I was joined by Tobe Hicks, who was going to Helena, Arkansas. As he had come but

47. The most likely rail route for Bevens to have traveled to Montgomery, Alabama, would have taken him southwest through Macon and Columbus, Georgia, and then west to Montgomery.

I have been unable to identify Tobe Hicks. His name does not appear in the census of 1860 for Arkansas or in the standard index to Arkansas soldiers.

48. Bevens's reference to Kingston is puzzling. Kingston is, indeed, about twenty miles from Selma, but it is northeast of the town, back toward Montgomery, and there was no rail connection there. Perhaps Bevens visited Kingston for some reason and means to say that he had to hurry back to Selma to catch the train. In any case, Meridian, Mississippi, is about a hundred miles west of Selma.

49. To reach Panola, Mississippi, Bevens would have had to make a ninety degree turn north at Jackson. It is difficult to say how far he traveled in three hours by railroad. With Jackson being only about eighty-five miles west of Meridian, he should have reached fairly near the town; yet he suggests that the train had not traveled very far from Meridian. It is also possible that the train reached and passed through Jackson on the way to Panola, but then was halted by a washed-out bridge over either the Pearl or Big Black rivers between Jackson and Panola, rather than between Meridian and Jackson. If Bevens had been forced to walk to Panola from very near Jackson, he would have had a journey of nearly 115 miles. The river he crossed at Panola was the Tallahatchee.

lately from the Trans-Mississippi army on some war business, and knew the route across the river, I decided to stick to him.[47]

We took a boat to Selma, on the Alabama river. There were many comrades on board and we passed the time in talking of the war. From Selma we went to Kingston, which was twenty-two miles from the railroad. We had to hurry to meet the train. We left at twelve o'clock and walked the ties to the junction, doing the twenty-two miles by seven o'clock. It was hard on Tobe Hicks. To our dismay we missed the train by five minutes and there was no other. We slept on the ground that night and next morning started on the hundred mile walk to Meridian.[48]

At Meridian we took the Jackson railroad, but had been on the train only three hours when we came to a wash-out bridge and had to walk again.

At Panola we gave a negro ten dollars to put us across the river in a skiff. Everywhere was water, water, water.[49]

When we could go no further we fell in with four men going down Cold Water on a flat boat with two bales of cotton. We told our tale of woe and they agreed to let us go with them if we would pull the boat. Although we had always lived on a river, we had never played deck hands. But this was no time to be dignified. We laid hold of the oars and played

50. The Coldwater, or Copasaw,
River merges with the Tallahatchee to
the north and west of Panola, so it is
impossible to say exactly where
Bevens made landfall.

deck hand for two days and a night. They were hard steamboat men. We could stand it no longer. Late in the afternoon Tobe said, "Let's land here." We landed and took off our traps. They tried to bully us into going on, but we were used to bluffs, and they couldn't work it.[50]

By walking ridges and wading sloughs, we came to the Mississippi. It was miles wide. We went to the house of a man whom Hicks knew. He told us the Yankees had patrol boats out every night and we would certainly be captured. We were between the devil and the deep blue sea. If we went back we would be captured; if we went on we would be captured. But danger had been our meat and drink for four years. We decided to build a raft of cedar logs, huge and square and long and light. We built it in a slough, back from the river, and when it was finished, we went to eat supper with this friend and bid him good-bye. Crossing the Mississippi at night on a raft could never be the safest journey in the world. With the Yankee patrol boat ready to capture us the danger was doubled.

But our friend said he knew of a man who had a skiff (if the Yankees had not burned it) that he would come for us if we could make him hear. We called and to our joy the fellow answered. He landed us at the mouth of St. Francis river about one o'clock in

51. Landing at the mouth of the St.
Francis River would have put Bevens
in Arkansas about seventy-five miles
east of Little Rock and just above
Helena.

the morning, and we gave him our watches and other valuables in payment for his services.[51]

We had to wade again, but we hurried on. At last we came to the parting of the ways, for Hicks was going to Helena and I to Jacksonport. We felt rather sad at separating after walking, wading, riding, playing deckhand and building rafts together.

To guide me Hicks gave me the names of all the men on the road who were o.k. About two o'clock in the morning I called up one of these o.k. men and asked to stay all night. He laughed and said, "It is day now."

I told him I had been up all night and must walk for my life that day. I must have two hours' sleep— on the floor, anywhere.

He told me the Yankees would capture me, but if they came I could run out the back door to the wood behind. He called me at four o'clock for a cup of coffee and a good breakfast, gave me nice lunch for noon, and I was walking on the slippery road before daylight. I walked for my life and made forty miles that day. When ready to pick out a place for the night I went to a house to find out where I was. The good woman saw that I was a rebel, and asked me what was my command.

"Cleburne's old Division, Govan's Brigade, Army of Tennessee," I answered.

She burst out crying, "For God's sake go on," she said, "Last night they captured my son from the same command."

I declared I was not tired at all, and had a half hour more of daylight anyhow. She told me how to get off the big road and where to stay all night. I went five miles further and when I asked for a night's lodging the good citizen had to be shown my furlough. Then he was glad to see me, gave me a fine supper and a good bed, and went with me next morning to show me the short cuts.

That day I went through the prairie, nine miles of sage grass. All day it poured rain, rain, rain. When about half way across there came a terrific cloudburst and I was nearly drowned. I thought, "Oh, to think that, after my perilous crossing of the great Mississippi, I should be drowned on a prairie so near home." I held my blanket over my head and out in front of me, so that I could breathe, and that saved me. Before I got to the next house I poured the water out of my boots and washed my socks. I pulled off my pants and washed them. I did this because I was afraid the family would not let such a muddy straggler stay all night. But they were nice to me.

I resumed my journey at daybreak. Bayou Deview was out of its banks. I waded to the channel, waist deep. I do not know how long I was about it, but I

52. Dr. Gray is probably William F. Gray of St. Francis County. According to the census of 1860, he was born in Alabama and owned a plantation worth nearly seven thousand dollars.

53. Judge Bevens was William C. Bevens, born in South Carolina about 1810 and the brother of Bevens's father. He had emigrated to Texas from South Carolina before settling at Batesville in 1846. A lawyer by profession, he served in the state legislature from 1852 to 1853 and was elected judge of the Third Judicial District in 1856. He died at Little Rock in September 1865. *Biographical and Historical Memoirs of Northeast Arkansas* (Chicago: Goodspeed Publishing Company, 1889), 644.

54. James M. Howell was born in Arkansas about 1837. He was serving as deputy sheriff in Jackson County when the war started. According to the census of 1860, he lived in the household of A. H. Logan, who was the county sheriff (1856–62) and the brother of Shannon Logan. Howell married eighteen-year-old Octavia Westmoreland of Woodruff County, in January 1864. Foster, *Marriage and Divorce Records,* 55.

finally got across and saw the sand ridges and the big home road.

I had to cross Cache river at Gray's Ferry. As a boy I had known Dr. Gray but he did not know me.[52] I went to the house, introduced myself, and showed him my furlough. He asked when I crossed the Mississippi. I told him. Had I walked all the way? I told him I had. Was I any relation of Judge Bevens of that district? I told him Judge Bevens was my uncle.[53] He finished by saying, "You have walked all the way from St. Francis river and have not stolen a horse?" I told him I was a gentleman, not a horse thief. He said, "Certainly, I will put you across the Cache river." He called to a negro to bring two horses, and we rode about a mile, to the ferry. There a man met us with a skiff and took me across. I went on my way and began to know the landmarks. When I reached the fork of the roads, (one leading to Augusta; the other to Jacksonport), I sat down to rest. Jim Howell, the deputy sheriff rode up. He looked at me for a minute, then shouted, "Why, is that you, Bill Bevens, what in hell are you doing here?"[54]

I showed him my furlough and told him about my journey. He made me ride, while he walked to his house, a few miles up the road. Then he put a little negro up behind me to ride some miles further.

I met Bill Campbell, who lost a leg at Shiloh. He wanted me to stay and talk, but I was headed for

55. I have been unable to identify Bill Campbell. Eighteen William Campbells resided in Arkansas in 1860, but none can be matched to the standard index to Arkansas soldiers.

56. Col. M. B. McCoy was born in South Carolina about 1812. According to the census, he was worth over ninety thousand dollars in 1860. His nineteen-year-old daughter, Ladona E. McCoy, had married James Bruce Waddill in August 1864. Foster, *Marriage and Divorce Records,* 109.

57. Bevens's sister, Sarah Kellogg, with whom he had been living when the war started, had three daughters, Eva, Nelly, and Emma, ages eleven, nine, and seven.

58. Independence County, where Bevens's parents still lived at Batesville.

home and would not stop.[55] I went on to Colonel McCoy's at Tupelo. I spent the night with Bruce Waddill. He lost a leg at Shiloh. It was the first time I had seen him since I helped carry him off the field. It was a happy meeting, and we talked nearly all night. He sent a little negro with me to Village Creek. I crossed in a canoe and walked the rest of the way— six miles—to Jacksonport.[56]

Home again! Was it only four years ago that the Jackson Guards had marched to the Presbyterian church to receive its banner from loving hands? How many miles we had traveled. How many battles we had fought. How many wretched homes and blazing cities we had seen. The sorrows, wounds, sufferings and deaths of centuries were crowded into those four years. Oh, the pity of it!

I went straight to my sister's home. Her little girls were dressed in long clothes, "playing lady." Their mother was at a neighbor's and one of them went for her, not telling her why she was wanted at home. Her surprise at seeing me was great, and our meeting joyous beyond words.[57]

She and the children went with me to father's home in the next county.[58] My mother had not heard from me, and she did not know whether I was alive or dead. She fell on my neck, cried, laughed, shouted. She almost died of joy. Father was too happy, and too full for utterance.

59. The war was, in fact, not over just because Gen. Robert Edward Lee (1807–70) surrendered the Army of Northern Virginia to Gen. Ulysses Simpson Grant (1822–85) at Appomattox, Virginia, on April 9, 1865. The First Arkansas, as part of Joe Johnston's command, did not surrender to General Sherman until April 27, at Greensboro, North Carolina. Some Confederate units farther west did not surrender until May or June.

60. Ezeriah F. Haggerton, a farmer, enlisted as a twenty-one year-old private in the Jackson Guards. He spent part of the war assigned to the Pioneer Corps. Haggerton occasionally got into trouble with the army. In March 1863, he forfeited six months' pay for being absent without leave at Bridgeport, Alabama. In January–February, 1864, he was confined to the guard house at Dalton, Georgia. Service Records, Roll 48.

61. By the time Bevens arrived back in Jackson County, some time in early April, his neighbors had felt the full weight of the war. Hunger was a particular problem. "I knew families," recalled one resident, "who lived six weeks during the spring of 1865 on bark from Elm trees, . . . We had scant food, hunger was not satisfied." Bevens would write elsewhere, "By 1865, those of us who returned at all, returned to find our properties destroyed, ourselves with no money and no jobs, and all our friends in the same condition. Every one had to start at the bottom." Sallie Walker Stockard, *The History of Lawrence, Jackson, Independence and Stone Counties of the Third Judicial District of Arkansas* (Little Rock: Arkansas Democrat Company, 1904), 71; William E. Bevens, "Makers of Jackson County: Short Stories of Early Pioneers, and Something about the Founding of Old Jacksonport," eds. Lady Elizabeth Luker and James Logan Morgan, *Stream of History* 21 (March 1984), 26.

Federal forces already controlled most of the state when news of Lee's surrender reached Little Rock on April 12. Merriwether Jeff Thompson, a native Virginian who became known as the "Swamp Fox of the Confederacy" for his partisan activities in the Trans-Mississippi theater, commanded the remnants of Confederate troops in the state. Thompson apparently held no official commission from either Arkansas or the C.S.A., but he claimed the rank of brigadier general. He surrendered to Lt. Col. Charles W. Davis, assistant provost marshal for the department commanded from St. Louis by Maj. Gen. John Pope, on May 9. Thereupon Thompson issued General Order No. 8, which directed all Confederate troops east of the Cache River and east of the White River south of the mouth of the Cache to assemble for parole at Wittenburg on May 25; troops west of the Cache and White rivers were to assemble at Jacksonport on June 5. Nearly six thousand men surrendered and were paroled at Jacksonport on June 5, including

Mother would look at me for hours and could not talk for joy. Her dear soul was never happier than now with her dear soldier boy safe at home, surrounded by loved ones. God gives no boy a better heritage than such a sweet Christian home and such love.

With her boy a thousand of miles away, and no mails, her prayers for him were the only connecting links. The boy on the field of death remembered his mother's prayers and was comforted in every danger.

I was unaccustomed to sleeping in a house, and at first used to take my blanket to the yard, but mother could not stand that and I had to go back. My sisters would look under rocks and planks and in various hiding places and bring out my jewelry and other treasures which they had hidden from the Yankees.

Before my furlough was out came the news of General Lee's surrender at Appomattox. The long cruel war was over and I was separated no more from my home and mother.[59] At Jacksonport I met the boys who had been furloughed with me, but had reached home first—John R. Loftin, Forrest Dillard, Haggerton and others.[60] It was good to be with the old comrades once more. We took up our work again. I began selling drugs. I married here and am still in Jackson county, at Newport, Arkansas.[61]

Bevens and, according to their service records, five other members of Company G: Peter Bach, James Hudson, William H. Hunter, John R. Loftin, and John L. McKee. Benjamin B. Bradley, also of Company G, signed his parole at Jacksonport on May 11. Michael B. Dougan, *Confederate Arkansas: The People and Policies of a Frontier State in Wartime* (University, Ala.: University of Alabama Press, 1976), 123–26; "Chronological History of the Civil War in Jackson County," *Stream of History* 3 (April 1965), Appendix 9–10; Lady Elizabeth Watson, *Fight and Survive!* (Conway, Ark.: River Road Press, 1974), 141–49; OR, vol. 48, pt. 2, 1298; Paroled Prisoner Rolls 1–226, Jacksonport, Arkansas [June 5] 1865, War Department Collection of Confederate Records, Record Group 109, National Archives. For Thompson see Jay Monaghan, *Swamp Fox of the Confederacy; the Life and Military Service of M. Jeff Thompson* (Tuscaloosa, Ala.: Confederate Publishing Company, 1956); Adele Graham, "'And Strike Again Tomorrow'" *Civil War* 8 (November–December 1990), 58–64.

Left to Right:
Thad Kinman,
Ed Dickinson,
Ben Adler
*These were my
friends who gave
me good clothes
instead of common,
regulation clothes.
They belonged to the
Quartermaster's
Department.*

Appendix

Muster Roll

The following is an alphabetical listing of all known members of Company G, First Arkansas Infantry. Names are spelled as they appear in *Compiled Service Records of Confederate Soldiers Who Served in Organizations from Arkansas,* with any variant spelling by Bevens provided in brackets. The rank indicated is the highest rank achieved. The symbols show what happened to individuals who left the company before the conclusion of the war. All who suffered wounds are identified.

Baber [Baker], George W., Private (t)
Baber [Baker], William H., Private (d)
Bach, Peter, Sergeant
Baird, John M. W., Corporal (w)
Baldridge, Alexander W., Private
Baldridge, John J., Private (w)
Barnes, William T., Musician (w)
Bedwell, James K., Private (y)

Berry, M. P., Musician (w) (d)

Bevens, William E., Corporal (w)

Bobo, James K., Private (w)

Bond, Robert D., Private (w) (c)

Bradley, Benjamin B., Private

Bradley, James A. M. D., Musician (w) (c)

Brogden [Bragden], Theophilus H., Private (k)

Bunnell, William, Private

Burnett, Casper K., Private

Burnett, Edward, Private (w) (k)

Byler, Tyre A., Corporal (x)

Carpenter, John, Private (d)

Cathey, John A., Private (w)

Choate, Austin, Private (w) (d)

Clayton, Willis H., Private (w) (y)

Clements, Henry C., Lieutenant

Collins, Finley, Private (k)

Dale, Eli V. B., Private (k)

Davis, Allen W., Sergeant (w) (k)

Davis, Thomas B., Sergeant (w) (y)

Dempsey, Edward, Private (y)

Densford, William B., Sergeant (d)

Dickson, Grandison F., Private (t)

Dillard, Forrest W., Corporal

Dorsey, Richard, Private (w) (x)

Dowell, Clifton W., Private (w)

Dye, Marion, Private

Ferrell, Benjamin H., Private (d)

Franks, Aaron B., Private (w) (c)

Frazier, James F., Private (d)

Fulcher [Falcher], James F., Private (d)

Garrett, James C., Private (t)

Gause, Lucien Cotesworth, Lieutenant (t)

Gause, Sidney S., Private (t)

Gill, Lyman B., Sergeant

Green, Arthur P., Private (k)

Haden, Richard M., Private (w) (t)

Haggerton, Ezeriah F., Private

Hamilton, John Joseph, Private (w) (t)

Harl, John E. A., Private (k)

Harl, Robert A., Private

Harrison, Jonathan H., Private (w) (d)

Hays, Daniel, Private (d)

Hensley, James M., Sergeant (k)

Henson, William H., Private (y)

Hiett [Heitt], John D., Private (x)

Howard, Martin A., Private (w) (t)

Hubbard, Joseph, Private (c)

Hudson, James, Private

Hunter, James F., Sergeant (t)

Hunter, William H., Private (x)

Jarrett, William H., Private (d)

Joslin, Joseph J., Private (w) (t)

Kinman, Doctor Frank, Private (x)

Lax, Joel T., Private (y)

Loftin, John R., Sergeant

Logan, Alonzo Rankin, Private (d)

Logan, Thomas Shannon, Corporal (w) (c)

Love, Jerry [D.], Private (c)

Love, John D., Private (d)

Love, Nathan, Private

Lowe, Henry Clay, Lieutenant (w)

McClain [McLain], John M., Private (k)

McCowan, Benjamin F., Private (w) (x)

McCullough, David, Private (t)

McDonald, John Alex, Private (w)

McKee, John Lemuel, Private (w) (d)

Marsden, Andrew P., Private (d)

Mathews, William M., Private (w) (d)

May, Jasper W., Private (w) (d)

Moore, John, Private (t)

Moore, Lucius L., Lieutenant (d)

Moore, William H., Private (k)

Mooreland, John, Private (x)

Morris, Robert, Private (x)

Mull, Martin A., Sergeant

Murphy, John K., Private (d)

Murphy, John M., Private (w) (c)

Murphy, William K., Private (d)

Murphy, Zebulon D., Private (d)

Myers, George D., Private (w) (d)

Myers, William A., Musician (x)

Nash, Michael C., Private

Orrick [Orric], John, Private (y)

Paine, George N., Lieutenant (d)

Pickett, Alexander Corbin, Captain (t)

Pinkley, William R. [P.], Private (k)

Porter, John, Private (x)

Powell, Henry, Private (w) (x)

Pritchard [Prichard], James H. P., Private (d)

Ramey [Raney], George W. [A.], Private (d)

Ratcliff, Jesse H., Private (w) (x)

Reagor [Reager], Anthony W. [G. W.], Private

Reardon [Readen], John W., Private (d)

Reaves [Reeves], Fountain M. [B. F.], Private

Reid [Reed], William H. C., Private (w)

Rhodes, Arthur, Private (d)

Rice, George W., Private (x)

Richardson, B. Frank, Private

Ridley, Young L., Sergeant

Roberts, George Washington, Private (t)

Roberts, Josiah R., Private (w) (d)

Robinson, John W., Private (x)

Roby, David A., Private (w) (x)

Rogers [Rodgers], John M. C., Private

Roy, Frederick, Private (c)

Sample, Joshua [Joseph], Private (d)

Shackleford, William D., Private (t)

Shoup, Samuel, Captain (w)

Slaughter, Owen [R.] L., Private (d)

Smith, Henry, Private (d)

Sparling, George, Sergeant

Steadman, Charles W., Private (k)

Steadman, Leonidas, Private

Steadman, Martin Luther, Private (x)

Stephens, George K., Private (d)

Stewart, Alfred, Private (k)

Stimson [Stinson], James W. [M.], Corporal (w) (k)

Stone, Thomas R., Private (t)

Thomas, George P., Sergeant (w) (k)

Trail, John B., Private (d)

Vanderford [Vanderfer], Beley P. [F]., Private (w)

Vaughn, Jasper [Joseph], Private (w) (d)

Waddill [Waddell], James B., Private (w) (d)

Waddill [Waddell], John M., Corporal (d)
Walthall, Allie T., Lieutenant (k)
Watts, John, Private (w) (x)
White, Benjamin F., Private (x)
Whitely, James H., Private (x)
Williams, William Fletcher, Private (w)
Williard, Beverly, Private (x)
Wilson, John, Private (y)
Winningham [Winneham], Daniel Boone, Private (x)
Winningham [Winneham], Harrison, Private (y)
Young, Rawlings, Surgeon

The following men are included on Bevens's roster of Company G, but their service cannot be verified by official records:

Boiler, John, Private
Conn, Jack, Private (d)
Cooper, William, Private (y)
Covey, B. L., Private
Ferrell, J. F., Private
Harl, Lou, Private
Kelley, David, Private (y)
Lamb, John, Private
Love, Wilson, Private
McCartney, W. M., Private (d)
Mulligan, David, Private
Murphy, J. H., Private (d)
Murphy, Patrick, Private (d)
Sallivan, R. H., Private (d)
Seward, James, Private (d)
Sherr, J. H., Private

Stewart, Pony, Private (k)
Stringfellow, Eli, Private (d)
Tucker, N. M., Private (d)
Whitely, James H., Private
Winneham [Winningham?], W. D., Private

(c) Captured for duration
(d) Discharged
(k) Killed in action or died of wounds
(t) Transferred
(w) Wounded
(x) Deserted
(y) Died but not from combat

Bibliography

Primary Sources: Manuscripts

Bevens, William E. Memorandum Book. Courtesy of Mrs. Lady Elizabeth Luker.

Bush, Frederick W. Letters. Special Collections, Mullins Library, University of Arkansas, Fayetteville.

Jones, Joseph Hubbard. Memoir. Special Collections, Mullins Library, University of Arkansas, Fayetteville.

Osbourne, Molsie A. R. Papers. Special Collections, Mullins Library, University of Arkansas, Fayetteville.

Stone, Thomas R., Diary. Arkansas History Commission, Little Rock.

Primary Sources: Newspapers

Atlanta Southern Confederacy
Augusta Chronicle and Sentinel
Arkansas Gazette
Milledgeville Confederate Union
Mobile Advertiser and Register

New York Times
Washington [Arkansas] *Telegraph*

Primary Sources: Public Documents

U.S. Census Bureau. Population Schedules [Free] of the Eighth United States Census, 1860, Arkansas. National Archives Microcopy No. 653, Rolls 37–52.

_____. Population Schedules [Slave] of the Eighth United States Census, 1860, Arkansas. National Archives Microcopy No. 653, Rolls 53–54.

U.S. War Department. Compiled Service Records of Confederate General and Staff Officers and Non-Regimental Enlisted Men. National Archives Microcopy No. 331.

_____. Compiled Service Records of Confederate Soldiers Who Served in Organizations from the State of Arkansas. National Archives Microcopy No. 317, Rolls 46–52.

_____. Index to Service Records of Confederate Soldiers Who Served in Organizations from the State of Arkansas. National Archives Microcopy No. 376.

_____. Paroled Prisoner Rolls 1–226, Jacksonport, Arkansas [June 5] 1865. War Department Collection of Confederate Records, Record Group 109, National Archives.

_____. *War of the Rebellion: A Compilation of the Official Records of the Union and Confederate Armies.* 70 vols. in 128 books and index. Washington: Government Printing Office, 1880–1901.

Primary Sources: Books and Articles

Beckham, Elihu C. "Where I Was and What I Saw During the War." *Stream of History* 18 (November 1979–July 1981), 3–20, and (November 1981), 23–43.

Bevens, William E. *Makers of Jackson County: Short Stories of Early Pioneers, and Something about the Founding of Old Jacksonport.* Newport, Ark.: Privately printed, 1923.

_____. "Makers of Jackson County: Short Stories of Early Pioneers, and Something about the Founding of Old Jacksonport." Eds. Lady Elizabeth Luker and James Logan Morgan. *Stream of History* 20 (December 1983), 19–36; 21 (March 1984), 7–27.

_____. *Reminiscences of a Private, Company "G," First Arkansas Regiment Infantry, May, 1861 to 1865.* Newport, Ark.: Lucien C. Gause Chapter No. 508, UDC, 1914.

_____. *Reminiscences of a Private, Company "G," First Arkansas Regiment Infantry, May, 1861 to 1865.* Newport, Ark.: Jackson County Historical Society, 1977.

_____. "Reminiscences of a Private." *Stream of History* 8 (July 1970), 45–52, (October 1970), 35–40; 9 (January 1971), 13–26, (April 1971), 33–40, (July 1971), 33–39, (October 1971), 29–39; 10 (January 1972), 23–39, (April 1972), 25–40.

Biographical and Historical Memoirs of Northeast Arkansas. Chicago: Goodspeed Publishing Company, 1889.

"Biographical Memoranda of Confederate Veterans of Jackson County, Arkansas." *Stream of History* 12 (July 1974), 3–32.

Clark, Walter, ed. *Histories of the Several Regiments and Battalions from North Carolina in the Great War 1861–'65.* 5 vols. Raleigh: E.M. Uzzell, 1901.

Confederate Veteran. 40 vols. Nashville, Tenn., 1893–1932.

Cowles, Calvin D., compl. *Atlas to Accompany the Official Records of the Union and Confederate Armies.* Washington: Government Printing Office, 1891–95.

Fenton, Charles A., ed. *Selected Letters of Stephen Vincent Benét.* New Haven: Yale University Press, 1960.

French, Samuel G. *Two Wars: an Autobiography.* Nashville: Confederate Veteran, 1901.

Harwell, Richard Barksdale, ed. *Kate: The Journal of a Confederate Nurse*. Baton Rouge: Louisiana State University, 1959.

Johnson, Robert Underwood and Clarence Clough Buell, eds. *Battles and Leaders of the Civil War*. 4 vols. New York: Century Company, 1887.

Luker, Lady Elizabeth, ed. "List of Confederate Soldiers Found in Old Ledger." *Stream of History* 5 (April 1967), 23–30.

McDonald, John. "Civil War Letter of John McDonald." *Stream of History* 2 (October 1964), 11–12. 16.

Morgan, James Logan, ed. *Directories of the Towns and Villages of Jackson County, Arkansas, June 1880*. Newport, Ark.: Privately printed, 1973.

_____. trans. *Independence County, Arkansas, Seventh Census Free Population Schedules 1850*. Newport, Ark.: Northeast Arkansas Genealogical Association, 1971.

Neill, Robert. "Reminiscences of Independence County." *Publications of Arkansas Historical Association* 3 (1911), 332–56.

Nichols, James L. and Frank Abbott, eds. "Reminiscences of Confederate Service by Wiley A. Washburn." *Arkansas Historical Quarterly* 35 (Spring 1976), 47–87.

"Return of Maimed Soldiers of Jackson County, Arkansas, 1867." *Stream of History* 13 (April 1975), 25.

Ross, Fitzgerald. *Cities and Camps of the Confederate States*. Ed. Richard Barksdale Harwell. Urbana: University of Illinois Press, 1958.

Scott, Joe M. *Four Years' Service in the Southern Army*. Mulberry, Ark.: Leader Office, 1897.

United Confederate Veterans of Arkansas, *ed. Confederate Women of Arkansas in the Civil War 1861–'65: Memorial Reminiscences*. Little Rock: H. G. Pugh, 1907.

Watkins, Sam R. *"Co. Aytch": A Side Show of the Big Show*. New York: Collier Books, 1962.

Williams, Charles G, ed. "A Saline Guard: The Civil War Letters of Col. William Ayers Crawford, C.S.A., 1861–1865." *Arkansas Historical Quarterly* 31 (Winter 1972), 328–55; 32 (Spring 1973), 71–93.

Wolf, John Q. "My Fifty Years in Batesville, Arkansas." Nancy Britton and Nana Farris, eds. *Independence County Chronicle* 23 (October 1981–January 1982), 1–49.

Woodruff, William E. *With the Light Guns in '61–'65: Reminiscences of Eleven Arkansas, Missouri and Texas Light Batteries in the Civil War.* Little Rock: Central Printing Company, 1903.

Worley, Ted R., ed. *They Never Came Back: The War Memoirs of Captain John W. Lavender, C.S.A.* Pine Bluff, Ark.: The Southern Press, 1956.

Secondary Sources: Books and Articles

Allen, Desmond Walls, compl. *Index to Arkansas Confederate Soldiers.* 3 vols. Conway, Ark.: D. W. Allen, 1990.

Bergeron, Arthur W. *Guide to Louisiana Confederate Military Units 1861–1865.* Baton Rouge: Louisiana State University Press, 1989.

Biographical Directory of the American Congress, 1774–1971. Washington: Government Printing Office, 1971.

Boatner, Mark M. III. *The Civil War Dictionary.* Revised ed. New York: David McKay Company, 1988.

Bonner, James C. *Milledgeville: Georgia's Antebellum Capital.* Athens: University of Georgia Press, 1978.

Bonner, Kathryn Rose, ed. *Arkansas 1860 U. S. Census Index.* Marianna, Ark.: Kathryn R. Bonner, 1984.

Britton, Nancy and Diane Tebbetts. "Nineteenth Century Homes of Batesville." *Independence County Chronicle* 20 (January 1979), 3–79.

Bryan, T. Conn. *Confederate Georgia.* Athens: University of Georgia Press, 1953.

Buck, Irving A. *Cleburne and His Command*. Jacksonville, Tenn.: McCowat-Mercer Press, 1959.

"Chronological History of the Civil War in Jackson County." *Stream of History* 3 (April 1965), Appendix 1–10.

Coggins, Jack. *Arms and Equipment of the Civil War*. New York: Fairfax Press, 1983.

Collier, Calvin L. *First In—Last Out: The Capitol Guards, Arkansas Brigade*. Little Rock: Pioneer Press, 1961.

Connelly, Thomas Lawrence. *Army of the Heartland: The Army of Tennessee, 1861–1862*. Baton Rouge: Louisiana State University Press, 1967.

_____. *Autumn of Glory: The Army of Tennessee, 1862–1865*. Baton Rouge: Louisiana State University Press, 1971.

Corley, Florence Fleming. *Confederate City: Augusta, Georgia, 1860–1865*. Columbia: University of South Carolina Press, 1960.

Coulter, E. Merton. *The Confederate States of America 1861–1865*. Baton Rouge: Louisiana State University Press, 1950.

Cozzens, Peter. *No Better Place to Die: The Battle of Stones River*. Urbana: University of Illinois Press, 1990.

Cunningham, H. H. *Doctors in Gray: The Confederate Medical Service*. Baton Rouge: Louisiana State University Press, 1958.

Davis, William C. *Battle at Bull Run: A History of the First Major Campaign of the Civil War*. Garden City: Doubleday & Company, 1977.

Dillard, Tom W. and Michael B. Dougan, compls. *Arkansas History: A Selected Research Bibliography*. Little Rock: Department of Arkansas Natural and Cultural Heritage, 1984.

Dougan, Michael B. *Confederate Arkansas: The People and Policies of a Frontier State in Wartime*. University, Ala.: University of Alabama Press, 1976.

Faust, Drew Gilpin. "Christian Soldiers: The Meaning of Revivalism in the Confederate Army." *Journal of Southern History* 53 (February 1987), 63–90.

Faust, Patricia L., ed. *Historical Times Illustrated Encyclopedia of the Civil War.* New York: Harper & Row, 1986.

Foster, Ardith Olene. *Marriage and Divorce Records of Jackson County, Arkansas, 1831–1875.* Newport, Ark.: Morgan Books, 1980.

Franke, Norman H. *Pharmaceutical Conditions and Drug Supply in the Confederacy.* Madison, Wis.: American Institute of the History of Pharmacy, 1955.

Freeman, Douglas Southall. *Lee's Lieutenants: A Study in Command.* 3 vols. New York: Charles Scribner's Sons, 1942–44.

Fulbright, Linda. "When Hairdressers Made Housecalls." *Independence County Chronicle* 13 (October 1971), 36–49.

Garrett, Franklin M. *Atlanta and Environs: A Chronicle of Its People and Events.* 3 vols. Athens: University of Georgia Press, 1969–87.

Govan, Gilbert E. and James W. Livingood. *A Different Valor: The Story of General Joseph E. Johnston, C.S.A.* Indianapolis: Bobbs-Merrill Company, 1956.

Graham, Adele. "'And Strike Again Tomorrow.'" *Civil War* 8 (November–December 1990), 58–64.

Hammock, John C. *With Honor Untarnished: The Story of the First Arkansas Infantry Regiment, Confederate States Army.* Little Rock: Pioneer Press, 1961.

Hattaway, Herman. *General Stephen D. Lee.* Jackson: University of Mississippi Press, 1976.

Hattaway, Herman and Archer Jones. *How the North Won: A Military History of the Civil War.* Urbana: University of Illinois Press, 1983.

Henry, Robert Selph. *"First with the Most" Forrest.* Indianapolis: Bobbs-Merrill, 1944.

Huddleston, Duane. "Morgan Magness Bateman was a Steamboatman." *Stream of History* 16 (January 1978), 3–32.

Hughes, Nathaniel Cheairs, Jr. *General William J. Hardee, Old Reliable.* Baton Rouge: Louisiana State University Press, 1965.

Jackson County Historical Society. *Dedication of Civil War Markers and Jacksonport State Park*. Jacksonport, Ark.: Jacksonport County Historical Society, 1965.

Jones, Joseph. "Roster of the Medical Officers of the Army of Tennessee." 22 *Southern Historical Society Papers* (1894), 165–280.

Krick, Robert K. *Lee's Colonels: A Biographical Register of the Field Officers of the Army of Northern Virginia*. Dayton, Ohio: Morningside Press, 1979.

Laux, Helen Marie. "James F. Hunter, Soldier and Builder." *Stream of History* 15 (January 1977), 19–22.

Leeper, Wesley Thurman. *Rebels Valiant: Second Arkansas Mounted Rifles (Dismounted)*. Little Rock: Pioneer Press, 1964.

Losson, Christopher. *Tennessee's Forgotten Warriors: Frank Cheatham and His Confederate Division*. Knoxville: University of Tennessee Press, 1989.

Luker, Lady Elizabeth. "Post Civil War Period in Jackson County." *Stream of History* 4 (October 1966), 31–38; 5 (January 1967), 19–27.

Luker, Lady Elizabeth. "The Surrender at Jacksonport." *Stream of History* 3 (April 1965), 5–6.

McDonald, Marjorie May, et al. *Souvenir Program presenting Glimpses and Highlights of the 135 Years of Jackson County History*. Newport, Ark.: Jackson County Historical Society, 1965.

McDonough, James Lee. *Five Tragic Hours: The Battle of Franklin*. Knoxville: University of Tennessee Press, 1983.

_____. *Shiloh—in Hell before Night*. Knoxville: University of Tennessee Press, 1977.

McMurry, Richard M. *John Bell Hood and the War for Southern Independence*. Lexington: University of Kentucky Press, 1982.

McWhiney, Grady. *Braxton Bragg and Confederate Defeat*. New York: Columbia University Press, 1969.

Madaus, Howard Michael and Robert D. Needham. *The Battle Flags of the Confederate Army of Tennessee*. Milwaukee: Milwaukee Public Museum, 1976.

Monaghan, Jay. *Swamp Fox of the Confederacy; the Life and Military Service of M. Jeff Thompson.* Tuscaloosa, Ala.: Confederate Publishing Company, 1956.

Moneyhon, Carl. "The Civil War and Socio-Economic Change in Jackson County, Arkansas." *Stream of History* 18 (November 1979–July 1981), 21–26.

Morgan, James Logan, ed. *Centennial History of Newport, Arkansas, 1875–1975.* Newport, Ark.: Jackson County Historical Society, 1975.

_____. *Families of Confederate Soldiers of Jackson County, Arkansas, 1861–1863.* Newport, Ark.: Morgan Books, 1982.

_____. *Genealogical Records of Independence County, Arkansas, 1845–1850.* Newport, Ark.: Northeast Arkansas Genealogical Association, 1972.

Parks, Joseph H. *General Leonidas Polk, C.S.A.: The Fighting Bishop.* Baton Rouge: Louisiana State University Press, 1962.

Purdue, Howell and Elizabeth. *Pat Cleburne, Confederate General.* Hillsboro, Tex.: Hill Junior College Press, 1973.

Roland, Charles P. *Albert Sidney Johnston: Soldier of Three Republics.* Austin: University of Texas Press, 1964.

Smith, Sidney Adair and C. Carter Smith, eds. *Mobile: 1861–1865. Notes and a Bibliography.* Chicago: Wyvern Press, 1964.

Stewart, Clyde, compl. "Independence County Officials 1820–1966." *Independence County Chronicle* 8 (January 1967), 12–19.

Stockard, Sallie Walker. *The History of Lawrence, Jackson, Independence and Stone Counties of the Third Judicial District of Arkansas.* Little Rock: Arkansas Democrat Company, 1904.

Sword, Wiley. *Shiloh: Bloody April.* New York: William Morrow & Company, 1974.

Thomas, Emory M. *The Confederate Nation: 1861–1865.* New York: Harper & Row, 1979.

Warner, Ezra J. *Generals in Blue: Lives of the Union Commanders.* Baton Rouge: Louisiana State University Press, 1964.

_____. *Generals in Gray: Lives of the Confederate Commanders*. Baton Rouge: Louisiana State University Press, 1959.

Watson, Lady Elizabeth. *Fight and Survive!* Conway, Ark.: River Road Press, 1974.

West, Mabel. "Jacksonport, Arkansas; Its Rise and Decline." *Arkansas Historical Quarterly* 9 (Winter 1950), 231–58.

Wigginton, Thomas A. et al. *Tennesseans in the Civil War: A Military History of Confederate and Union Units with Available Rosters of Personnel*. 2 vols. Nashville: Civil War Centennial Commission, 1964.

Williams, T. Harry. *P. G. T. Beauregard: Napoleon in Gray*. Baton Rouge: Louisiana State University Press, 1955.

Woods, James M. *Rebellion and Realignment: Arkansas's Road to Secession*. Fayetteville: University of Arkansas Press, 1987.

Woodward, C. Vann. ed, *Mary Chesnut's Civil War*. New Haven: Yale University Press, 1981.

Woodward, Mary Davis. "Dr. W. E. Arnold—A Personality Sketch." *Arkansas Historical Quarterly* 8 (Winter 1949), 331–35.

Woodworth, Steven E. *Jefferson Davis and His Generals: The Failure of Confederate Command in the West*. Lawrence: University of Kansas Press, 1990.

Index

Pillow, J. D., 205
Pine Bluff (Ark.), 118
Pine Mountain, 170–71
Pinter, Andrew J., 170
Pochahontas (Ark.), 82, 153
Polk, Leonidas, 98, 126–27, 155,
    164–65, 170–71
Polk, Lucius E., 112, 116, 118, 126,
    145, 146, 158, 160–61, 166, 168,
    170
Pool, M. J., 62
Pope, John, 250
Potomac River, 45–49, 55–57, 58
Powell, Samuel, 88, 98, 108–09
Powell River, 107
Prairie County (Ark.), 126
Prescott (Ark.), 86
Prices, 54–55, 154, 230–31, 234
Pulaski (Tenn.), 218–25
Pulaski County (Ark.), 156
Pumpkin Vine Creek, 168
Purcell's Battery, 36–41, 45, 56

Quintard, Charles T., 126–27

Railroad Gap, 125
Raleigh (N.C.), 232
Red Sulphur Springs, 89
Refugees, 237
Reid, William H. C., 63, 91–93
Reminiscences of a Private, xii–xiii,
    xv–xviii, xxii–xxiii, 6
Republican Party, xxv
Resaca (Ga.), 158–60, 200
Richmond (Ky.), 100–01
Richmond (Va.), 20–21, 23, 26, 30
Ringgold Gap, 146–50
Roberts, George W., 152–53
Roberts, Martha, 152
Roberts, Sarah, 72
Robinson, J., 72, 74
Robinson, John, 6–8

Robinson, Mrs. John, 6–8
Rock Spring Church, 132
Rocky Face Ridge, 158
Roll of Honor, 114
Rosecrans, William S., 112–13, 124,
    126, 128, 132, 138
Rossville (Ga.), 138
Rough and Ready (Ga.), 196
Roy, Thomas B., 120–21
Ruggles, Daniel, 30, 32, 62
Rutherford's Creek, 216

St. Francis County (Ark.), 246
St. Francis River, 241–43
Saline Guards, 14
Salt River, 96
Sand Mountain, 202–04
Savannah River, 232
Scales, William H., 66–67, 232
Schnable, John A., 10
Schnable's Battalion, 10
Schofield, John M., 155–56, 164,
    205–07, 213
Scott, Joe M., xiv
Scott, Thomas J., 84, 133
Scott, Winfield, 42–44
Secession, xxv–xxvii
Selma (Ala.), 238–39
Selvige, Sopronia C., 16
Semple's Battery, 142
Sequatchie Valley, 87, 138–39
Shackelford, William D., 34–35, 123
Shelbyville (Tenn.), 111–12
Sherman, William T., 143, 156, 168,
    170–71, 177, 185–87, 196–97, 202,
    230, 232, 250
Shiloh, 33, 63–64, 66–74, 76, 165
Shoup, J., 52
Shoup, Samuel, 17, 52–53, 62–63, 67,
    69, 71, 123, 129, 147, 182–83
Slaughter, Owen L., 122
Slavery, xxv, xxvii, 5–7, 154